Gunfire in Barbary

Admiral Lord Exmouth's battle
with the Corsairs of Algiers in 1816
–the story of the suppression of white
christian slavery by Roger Perkins and
Captain K J Douglas-Morris RN

Kenneth Mason

Gunfire in Barbary

The print overleaf shows the slave market at
Algiers. Tens of thousands of hapless
European captives passed through this
terrifying ordeal (British Museum)

The endpapers of this book show an
interview with Omar Bashaw, Dey of
Algiers, August 20, 1816. Left to right, Rear
Admiral Sir Charles Penrose, Abraham
Salamé, Omar Bashaw, and Captain Sir
James Brisbane. Behind them, the Admiral
of the Algerine fleet and the Captain
of the port of Algiers

Published by Kenneth Mason
Homewell, Havant, Hampshire
©Roger Perkins and Captain K Douglas-Morris RN 1982

British Library Cataloguing in Publication Data
Perkins, Roger
    Gunfire in Barbary
    1. Algiers — Bombardment, 1816
    I. Title II. Douglas-Morris, K.J.
    965'.302 DT299.A5

    ISBN 0-85937-271-5

Printed in Great Britain by
Redwood Burn Ltd Trowbridge Wiltshire
and designed by Geoff M Sadler MSIAD

ISBN 0-85937-271-5

Contents

PLYMOUTH SOUND FROM DEVIL'S POINT

Acknowledge-ments

IT WOULD BE IMPOSSIBLE to write a story as complex as 'Gunfire in Barbary' without the unstinting support of a large number of individuals and specialist organisations. The authors wish to express their gratitude to everyone who has assisted, in one way or another, in the production of this book. In particular, they must thank the administrators and staff of the Public Records Office (Kew), County Records Office (Truro and Exeter), Royal Marines Museum (Eastney), Royal Naval Museum (Portsmouth), Royal Artillery Institution (Woolwich), Royal Engineers Museum (Chatham), National Maritime Museum (Greenwich), British Museum (London), United States Navy Academy Museum (Annapolis), and Afdeling Maritieme Historie (Ministry of Defence, Den Haag). Much assistance was received also from Maggs Brothers Limited (London) and Devon Library Services.

Crown copywright records in the Public Records office appear by kind permission of Her Majesty's Stationery Office.

Of the many individuals involved, special thanks are due to Colin White MA for his expert guidance at every stage, to Clive Morris for his painstaking investigations at Gibraltar, and to Cdr F C van Oosten RNN for having so generously made available his profound knowledge of Dutch naval affairs. Vital assistance and information have been provided also by Peter Dale, Derek B Spalding, Max Powling, Richard Humble, Mrs Wenny Humble, Leonard Couzens, Geoffrey Whitehead, Julian Ahearne, Laurie Manton, Bob Scarlett, Geoff M Sadler, Lt Cdr Kenneth Burns RN (retd), Lt Cdr W J Schram de Jong RNN, and the present Viscount Exmouth.

Finally, the authors are indebted to their own families for their forbearance during the past five years of non-availability and creative ill-humour.

FOREWORD

& A man his medal

ON AUGUST 27, 1816, a combined Anglo-Dutch fleet bombarded the port and city of Algiers. For ten hours this North African stronghold was battered by one of the most ferocious cannonades ever directed against a land target by ship-borne artillery. The expenditure in munitions was enormous and several thousand men died that day. The fleet was commanded by one of England's greatest sailors, Admiral Lord Exmouth, better known to later generations as that dashing captain of frigates, Sir Edward Pellew. He emerged from the encounter victorious, but only by the narrowest of margins and having suffered a higher proportion of casualties than had Nelson at Trafalgar.

Despite the drama and violence of the encounter it remains one of the least known of the Royal Navy's many great actions during the age of sail. It is strange that this should be so. The battle of Algiers was fought under circumstances which were in many ways unique. Apart from the Battle of Navarino in 1827, this was the last action to be fought by a squadron of the Royal Navy propelled solely by sail. It was one of the few naval battles in which extensive use was made of rocket-launched missiles. It also involved various technical innovations in naval gunnery. These and other unusual aspects of the encounter qualify Algiers for a special place in maritime history.

One hundred and sixty-six years have passed since the roar of battle rolled around the shore-line hills of Algiers and, in all that time, no detailed account has been published. This book is a belated recognition of the skill and courage, on both sides, with which the battle was fought.

Lord Exmouth's attack was the culminating point in a story

which had started nearly three hundred years earlier when Emperor Charles V made the first attempt to suppress the slavers of the Barbary coast. The story is one which contains a strange mixture of elements: religious bigotry, commercial greed, racial prejudice, economic exploitation, and military incompetence. The bombardment of Algiers was a milestone in history. The Dutch and British sailors in Lord Exmouth's fleet fought and died there because it was inevitable that they should do so. The events of earlier decades had brought them to that place and at that time. It is for this reason that the following chapters must describe not only the battle itself but also the reasons for which it was fought.

Before launching into the task of describing the grand design, however, it is necessary to mention the fact that both authors of this book are medal collectors. The hobby of collecting medals is unlike most others in that the interest and pleasure derive not from simple pride of acquisition and ownership but from delving into the history of the object collected. In basic terms, a medal consists of nothing more than an ornately worked piece of gold, silver or bronze, suspended by a length of coloured ribbon. That which makes each medal unique is the personal story of the individual to

whom it was originally awarded. It is to the great benefit of the present-day collector and historian that medals awarded to members of the British armed forces, with rare exceptions, have been officially impressed or engraved with the individual recipient's rank and name. Hence it is possible to identify the man himself and the ships or regiments in which he served. With this information one may then go further and trace the full story of his service career, his part in various battles or campaigns and the place and manner in which he may have met his death. It was a routine enquiry into the military service of a nineteenth century soldier which in fact prompted the writing of this book.

In 1977 the authors were involved jointly in researching the life story of one Richard Parry. This man had been awarded the Naval General Service medal (1793-1840 series) with the clasp 'Algiers'. The award indicated that he had participated in the battle and had lived long enough subsequently to claim his entitlement. There was nothing unusual in any of this: the medal is relatively common in collecting circles. Initial research soon revealed, however, that there were two difficult aspects to Parry's medal. First, all documentary evidence of his existence had been apparently lost and, secondly, even though it was known that he had been a soldier, the archives gave no clear indication as to why a contingent of army personnel should have been included in Lord Exmouth's expedition.

The medal had passed down through successive generations of Richard Parry's descendants and for many years had been in the possession of Mr Norman Blewett of Newton Abbot in Devon. The Blewett family had inherited Parry's medal but had no specific information regarding his career. It was therefore necessary to examine public and county records in the hope of finding some reference to him. Patient detective work usually reaps its just reward and, after twelve months of frustration, the picture took shape. Richard Parry had been born in 1783 in Wendron,

When Richard Parry left his native county he cannot have imagined that his army service might bring him to the shores of Africa, under the command of a famous fellow Cornishman, and that together they would fight to destroy white Christian slavery (National Maritime Museum)

Cornwall, a small mining community dependent upon the local deposits of copper and tin. When big enough, at the age of eight or nine years, he followed his father and brothers in the trade of miner. In 1813, at the age of thirty, he left home and walked two hundred miles to Portsmouth where he enlisted in the Corps of Royal Sappers & Miners on December 21. He was five feet, four inches in height, of swarthy complexion, had brown hair and grey eyes, was illiterate, and had no previous military experience. Less than three years later he found himself aboard HMS *Impregnable* in the bay of Algiers, surrounded by death and destruction while the ship was pounded by the cannon and mortar fire of the port defences. He was lucky to survive the day unhurt.

Completing his engagement with the Sappers & Miners, Parry returned to Cornwall and settled in Treskerby, close to Gwennap. His death certificate shows that he died of old age on November 8, 1861, aged seventy-eight and still described as a copper miner. No doubt his grandchildren had many times heard the tale of his great fight, long ago and far away, with the fearsome pirates of Barbary.

The Parry project had been successful, but the search for his personal papers had produced more questions than answers on the much larger story of the Algiers affair itself. Numerous minor accounts of the battle had appeared over the years, but these dealt solely with the naval aspects. Earlier writers had largely ignored the escalation of pressures which made the bombardment necessary in the first place, and they did not examine its long-term effectiveness. Clearly there was a gap which needed to be filled in the historical record. Subsequently the small acorn of the Richard Parry story has germinated and grown. It has developed roots and branches, and these are the chapters in the whole complex story of Algiers, 1816.

CHAPTER ONE

Beware the terrible Turk!

FOR MORE THAN three hundred years the Turk was the bogeyman of Europe. He came in the night by stealth, he ravished women and carried off young children. Turbaned, bearded, armed with a glittering scimitar, he was a Satan in human form. The Turk was an alien, a murderous dark-skinned foreigner. He enslaved the helpless Christian for the indulgence of his own depraved and often unspeakable pleasures.

So ran the legend. It was, by any standard, an extraordinary reputation. The very name Turk caused fear and loathing. Why? Who were these people? What had they done to provoke such hatred? Did their exploits truly justify such a sense of evil?

The story of the Turks (and even that title is misleading) is a blend of truth and myth which became progressively distorted with the passing years. To understand the reality of their notoriety it is necessary to know something of their history and origins.

The Turks who feature in this story were, first and foremost, professional kidnappers. Their economic survival depended upon their ability to seize hostages and hold them to ransom. Their culture and way of life revolved around this basic fact, and their activities were based upon three ancient city sites in Barbary, that narrow ribbon of land which stretches nearly fifteen hundred miles from the Straits of Gibraltar to the Gulf of Sirte. Clinging to the northern fringe of the immense continent of Africa, this long strip of fertile coastline has witnessed some of the bloodiest episodes in human history. In the era when the Mediterranean basin constituted the whole of the known world, Barbary was as closely involved in man's destiny as the classical lands of Italy and Greece.

Long before the birth of Christ the area came to prominence with the growth of the great Carthaginian empire. A vigorous people, the Carthaginians expanded into southern Europe where, inevitably, they clashed with the Roman empire. The power struggle continued through the three Punic Wars and led to the eventual sacking of Carthage in 146 BC. The Romans occupied the area and the people of Barbary shared in Rome's conversion to Christianity. Roman civilisation took root in Africa and flourished. The conquerors exploited the natural fertility of the land, commerce thrived and the ports of Algiers, Tunis and Tripoli became important trading centres. For five hundred years there was peace and prosperity. Barbary was, in terms of language, law, religion and custom, an integral part of Europe.

With the collapse of Rome, and the shift of power eastward to Constantinople, the people of Barbary found themselves increasingly isolated. Disaster arrived in the form of invasion by the Vandals who swept down through France and Spain and crossed over to Africa at the Straits of Gibraltar. The invaders were gradually absorbed, adopting Christianity and turning their swords into ploughshares.

In the eighth century came the next invasion. The forces of Islam were on the march, carrying sword and flame to every point of the compass which their horsemen could reach. Barbary was colonised by the Arabs who then moved on, across the Straits and into Spain where they settled in Granada. Barbary was now no longer an area which looked to Europe for its affiliations; it was bound instead by Islamic custom, law and military strength to the East.

Barbary was ruled jointly during the twelfth, thirteenth and fourteenth centuries by the Arabs (descendants of the invaders), and by the Christians and the Jews and Armenians.

The fifteenth century witnessed the ascendancy of the Ottoman or Turkish Empire. Fired by the twin ambitions of carrying the Koran to new territories and of promoting their commercial activities at the same time, the hardy, capable Turks brought a fresh tide of invasion sweeping westward through the Mediterranean, southward into Egypt and northward into the Balkans. In those areas where Islam was already established, they gained power by treaty and alliance, as in Barbary. In areas where Christianity still survived, they found it convenient to maintain the *status quo*, as in Greece, parts of the Eastern Adriatic, and modern-day Lebanon.

By 1580 the city of Algiers had been provided with powerful defences. The landward batteries were neglected in later years, but the number of cannon covering the port increased steadily. Even so, a French squadron commanded by Admiral the Marquis Duquesne achieved some success in 1682. He launched a violent attack and redeemed many of his enslaved compatriots (National Maritime Museum)

In other areas they took up the sword and attempted fresh conquests. This was particularly the case in the Balkans where the Turks pressed continuously north-westward until finally stopped not far from Vienna by the Polish King Sobieski in 1683. That the Turks — orientals and Muslims — should have succeeded in reaching so far up into the heartland of Europe explains in part the fear and suspicion in which they were held by our forbears.

During the sixteenth and seventeenth centuries the Ottoman Empire was consolidated and developed. It reached its peak of power and influence during the reign of its greatest Sultan, Suleiman the Magnificent. The Ottoman Navy was re-organised and expanded by the brilliant Kheir-ed-Din Barbarossa, the man who in 1529 re-built the port of Algiers and transformed it into a naval fortress. These two remarkable men worked together so well that their fleet dominated the Mediterranean for many years.

For a time the Ottomans were invincible, but the Empire was too far-spread for it to remain permanently under the direct control of Constantinople. With the passing years and with continuing problems of communication, the more distant provinces were granted a measure of semi-autonomy. The Sultan appointed Pashas to govern the provinces on his behalf, granting the chosen men an edict of authority, but even this kind of mandate failed to

Although past the zenith of their power and influence, the Ottomans could still afford to maintain a magnificent lifestyle in Constantinople. This was the new palace, on the Bosphorous, of Sultan Mahmoud II who ruled from 1808 to 1839 AD

stand the test of time. Some of the Pashas failed to understand local problems, others were self-seekers, or were simply incompetent. It therefore became the custom for the furthest provinces of the Empire to elect their own leaders, the Deys, from the local populace, the appointments then being approved by the Sultan in Constantinople. The process of election was not always conducted in the best spirit of democracy.

Between 1450 and 1750, therefore, the Barbary Coast was a province of the Ottoman Empire, controlled by the Sultan but with the degree of control gradually weakening all the time. After 1750 that control disappeared almost entirely. Perhaps Tripoli, being geographically closer to Constantinople, had less independence than Algiers and Tunis which, in most respects, had been permitted to break away. However, there were still certain obligations which they were expected to meet, such as sending ships to assist the Turkish navy whenever it was involved in a war. The Sultan was consulted as a final arbiter in high-level disputes. He could still intervene if affairs in the Western Mediterranean were not in accord with his overall policy for the Empire. In the main, however, the Sultan was content to have the Barbary states as a friendly shield, protecting his Empire from any major incursion from the west by the Christian powers.

The nineteenth century saw an acceleration in the long decline of the Ottomans. Much of their North African territory was conquered and colonised by the European states. Italy took Tripoli, France took Tunis and Algiers, while Morroco remained in Spanish hands. It was only in the mid-twentieth century that the Europeans withdrew, leaving behind them the newly independent nations of Libya, Tunis and Algeria.

Today we speak of 'Algerians' as being the unified people of that country. Throughout this book the term 'Algerine' has been used in preference, partly because that was the description in use at the time of the battle but mainly as a continuing reminder that we are dealing here with a polyglot community of many different religious, racial and cultural backgrounds. Their loyalties were not based upon a simplistic 'one nation' patriotism. To the contrary, they were motivated by considerations, part religious but mainly commercial, which shaped the development of the Corsairs.

By the late sixteenth century the economy of Algiers was in decline. The fertility of the land was exhausted, the Roman irrigation systems were long derelict and the woodlands denuded.

Castle

The new Star Castle

MEDI T

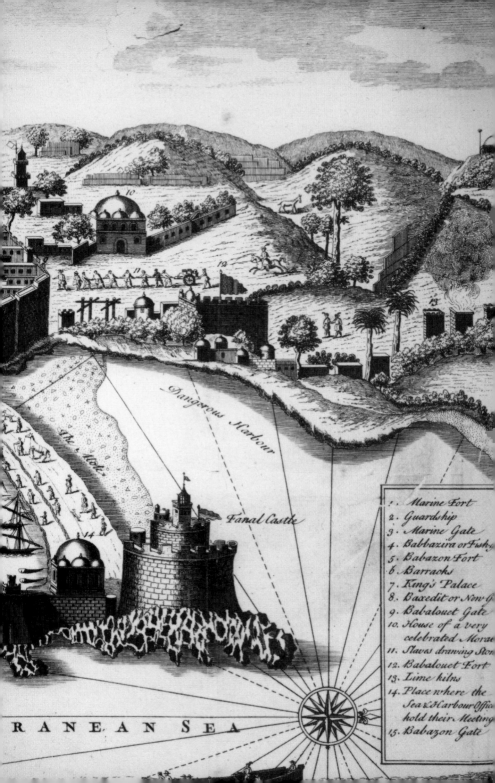

Dangerous Harbour

Fanal Castle

The Mole

RANEAN SEA

1. Marine Fort
2. Guardship
3. Marine Gate
4. Babbazira or Fish
5. Babazon Fort
6. Barracks
7. King's Palace
8. Baxedit or New G
9. Babalouet Gate
10. House of a very
    celebrated Mora
11. Slaves drawing Ston
12. Babalouet Fort
13. Lime kilns
14. Place where the
    Sea & Harbour Offic
    hold their Meeting
15. Babazon Gate

The future was bleak and there were no rooted traditions to encourage the idea of hard physical work to put things right. To the Algerines the solution was obvious: if they could not produce enough for their own needs then they must perforce seize that which belonged to others. And so was adopted a way of life based exclusively on robbery, ransom and enslavement. Licences were granted to the ablest captains and the long reign of terror began, the heydey of the Corsairs.

A Corsair was a professional sailor-raider, the word 'corso' meaning chase or pursuit. In principle it is wrong to describe such men as pirates. The act of piracy occurs when robbery is committed at sea, or by attack from the sea, by people who have not been granted any formal authority by a recognised state to commit that act. The granting of a letter of marque, signed by a head of state or one of his delegated officers, gave legality to the robbery. Provided that he operated within the limitations set out in his licence, the captain could claim that he was practising his profession, not committing a crime. This was an age-old practice, certainly much in favour with the English, many of whose most famous heroes went privateering against the Spanish treasure ships in the Caribbean and South America and much to the benefit of Queen Elizabeth's exchequer.

Initially the Corsairs of Barbary combined with the Sultan's forces from the Eastern Mediterranean to wage full-scale war upon the Christian states such as Venice and Genoa. These were very large expeditions involving hundreds of ships and thousands of men. Powerful forces were put ashore to attack the enemy's towns and cities, to sack and seize immense treasures and to carry off thousands of prisoners. This phase soon passed and the Corsairs settled into the role which they were to maintain for three hundred years. Apart from sea-raiding every summer season, this consisted of rapid minor attacks upon the smaller Christian towns and villages.

These places were not well fortified and were defended by local militia who, given the chance, and at the first sign of trouble,

Preceding page: the main features of Algiers are shown clearly in this beautiful sketch by an unknown English artist. By the time Exmouth launched his attack, many decades after the picture was published, the defences had been made even more powerful (British Museum)

Corsair galleys terrorised the Mediterranean shipping lanes throughout the 16th and 17th centuries. Armed with a single bow chaser and forty fighting Janissaries, they were ideal for limited forays lasting a few weeks during each summer cruising season (British Museum)

would head for the hills in company with the local population. There was no community anywhere around the coasts of the Western Mediterranean which could not be reached by the Corsairs of Barbary, and every such community, generation after generation, was obliged to maintain a night and day watch against sudden assault. To these Christians the raiders from the sea were known under one dreaded collective name — 'the Turks'. Their reputation spread far beyond the confines of the Western Mediterranean and so did their privateering activities. As more and more renegade European sailors rose to high rank in the Corsair fleet, so did the audacity of the raiders increase. A *Rais* (Captain) who had learned to navigate around his home country's coastline of England or France could with confidence sail back some years later and raid the area where he had been raised as a boy or young man.

The traditional lateen-rigged vessels of Barbarossa's navy were unsuited for these distant water cruises. The cold northern seas demanded a sturdier design. It is ironic that the solution to the problem was provided by an Englishman, Captain John Ward of Faversham, and a Dutchman, Captain Simon Danser of Dordrecht. These two adventurers each made their way to Barbary in the early years of the sixteenth century and they provided an impetus to the expansion of Corsair activities by introducing the square-rigged round ship. Sailing from Tunis and Algiers, they led numerous forays against European shipping and taught European methods of navigation and seamanship to the local *Rais*. Both men amassed large personal fortunes before meeting untimely ends (Ward died of fever at Tunis and Danser was beheaded by the Dey of that city). However, it was their dubious honour to have set an example which was copied with enthusiasm by the *Rais* of Barbary.

Corsair raids upon the coasts of Madeira, Portugal, France, Spain, England and Denmark became common-place. In 1627 they successfully raided the Irish coast. In 1654 they captured a fishing village in Cornwall. Their ships cruised every summer in the Bristol Channel, the English Channel and the Thames Estuary. During the reign of King Charles II a standing order to British warships was that they 'should keep a sharp look-out for Turks men-of-war in the Channel'. Fear of these ships reached such proportions that special prayers were included in some church services. An entry in the churchwarden's accounts for the parish of St Helen's, Abingdon, reads, 'Anno MDLXV, 8 of

A rare pitched battle in the 17th century between heavily armed ships of the Dutch navy and lateen-rigged galleys. The Corsairs normally relied upon surprise and guile (National Maritime Museum)

Queen Elizabeth, payde for two bokes of Common Prayer agaynst invading of the Turks, sixpence'.

The Barbary Corsairs were interested in one thing above all else — they went raiding for prisoners. They were moderately interested in 'treasure' in the conventional sense of that word and would welcome certain kinds of cargo, provided that it had a high value and did not take up too much space. They would often keep a prize ship and sail it back to their home port if it were of a type suitable for stripping and converting as a future Corsair vessel. In many instances, however, the seized ships were too large and cumbersome for such work and these were either sold or sunk. The ambition of every *Rais* was to return to port with his ship pressed low in the water by the weight of as many human beings as he could cram into her hull. Prisoners were equated with profit.

The Corsair ships of Barbary were fundamentally no different in design from the privateer vessels operating elsewhere around the world. To achieve success, however, they needed to meet certain basic criteria: small and handy, large enough for open-sea cruising, small enough to be unobtrusive, sufficient accommodation to hold a strikeforce of fighting men, relatively shallow draft for coastal

The Corsairs were not always successful. Here a Royal Navy boarding party, armed with cutlasses, storms the maindeck of an Algerine cruiser (National Maritime Museum)

work, and stable enough to carry prisoners and looted cargoes. Such ships did not need to be heavily armed. They relied upon speed and surprise to run alongside a victim, board her and overwhelm the crew. A broadside-to-broadside duel was always disastrous for a privateer. To achieve speed and responsive handling, these small ships sacrificed the thickness of heavy timber needed to resist cannon-balls. The Corsairs were fitted with light swivel guns which could send a blast of grape-shot across the deck of a particularly reluctant victim, but this happened very rarely. Nearly always the sight of a rapidly closing Corsair was enough to frighten the merchantman's crew and passengers into submission. Victims spoke afterwards of the terror caused by the noise of the boarders who screamed, shouted, beat drums and clashed their scimitars on shields.

Surprise was achieved in a number of ways. A Corsair would hide in the lee of any small island used by merchantmen as a navigational reference point, and then race out and lay alongside in a matter of moments. She might approach down-sun in the evening, making it difficult for the victim to identify her. The Rais would hide his fighting men below decks, fly the same colour as his intended victim, approach within hailing distance, lull the suspicions of the target ship and then suddenly close in. There was always someone aboard the Corsair ship who had as his mother tongue the language of any crew likely to sail through the Mediterranean. This man would hail the victim and engage in friendly conversation while the Rais was preparing to pounce. On other occasions prize ships were used as decoys. The Corsair captain relied upon such ruses to claim a quick conquest rather than risk being knocked to pieces by a heavier opponent.

Corsair ships were propelled not only by sail but also, very often, by sweeps or oars. This gave them two advantages: they could produce a high turn of speed for short distances and they could run down a victim which was becalmed or moving too slowly to escape. The dual method of propulsion created one particular problem for the Rais: when leaving port for a cruise of forty to sixty days he was obliged to carry food and water for the galley slaves, for the crew, and also for captured prisoners. As a result, the standard of messing and accommodation was extremely primitive. Many prisoners complained of their harsh treatment aboard a Corsair ship but, in fact, they were often as well-treated in this respect as the ship's own crew.

A typical Algiers street scene. The artist has not exaggerated the size of the fetters, some weighed 50 kgs. At the height of their power, the Algerines held as many as 25,000 white slaves in captivity. Over-crowding of the bagnios and over-loading of the water and sewerage systems brought frequent epidemics of bubonic plague, typhoid and cholera (British Museum)

It was not always so. There is convincing proof that many victims were treated with appalling harshness. Eye-witness accounts tell of the excited Algerines swarming aboard and immediately stripping their captives naked. The captain would be beaten on the soles of his feet, the torture of the *bastinado*, to force him into revealing the hiding place of any treasure aboard and to name the wealthiest passengers liable to yield the highest ransom. Victims who had swallowed their jewellery or concealed it in their body orifices were liable to be cut open or thrown overboard. Like locusts, the attackers stripped the vessel of every item of value before putting it to the torch or setting sail with a prize crew.

When a Corsair returned to port, laden with prisoners and possibly escorting one or more prize ships, the people of the town congregated at the dock to see how successful the *Rais* had been. If the cruise was financed by the Dey, his officers would go aboard for a report and an accounting of the spoils. If it had been a private venture, financed by one or more bankers and merchants, they too were anxious to know the result of their investment. The *Rais* would give them an inventory of the prisoners, stating their names, origins, wealth, importance, and other details which established their relative value as hostages.

Disembarked near-naked and in chains, the prisoners were taken to a quarantine barracks. Bubonic plague was endemic and great care was taken to ensure that this and other diseases were not brought ashore from captured ships. After quarantine, the prisoners were taken to the slave market for auction, the men being inspected in public by prospective buyers to see if they were fit and sound. An ailing hostage might die before ransom was paid. The basis of investment was, first, the amount and quality of work expected to be obtained during the period of slavery and, secondly, the amount of ransom to be negotiated. In this way the purchaser was acquiring a commodity which, hopefully, would prove to be a sound investment with a reasonably rapid return on his capital outlay. For those men who had limited prospects of being ransomed the physical examination was a test of their fitness to withstand many years of arduous physical work. Women were examined privately in a building set aside for that purpose. Once purchased, the prisoners were held in large buildings known as *bagnios* where they remained permanently or to which they were returned each evening after their day's work. Conditions in the *bagnios* varied considerably from one town to another. Some were reasonably sanitary and well administered, others were grossly overcrowded and squalid, comparable with the worst of the debtor's jails in nineteenth century England. They were undoubtedly miserable places. While he lay in the *bagnio*, trying to adjust to his new and alien surroundings, the unhappy prisoner's fate was being decided by an elaborate network of intermediaries who commenced negotiations regarding the ransom. Discussions were held at various levels and through various channels, depending upon the importance and the nationality of the hostage concerned.

Most of the European powers maintained consulates in the three main Barbary ports. Part of their function was to intercede on behalf of the individual wealthy prisoners, negotiate block payments for groups of less important prisoners, and to guarantee the payment of tribute due from their own governments. Also present in each city were groups of Redemptionist Fathers, monks from Rome, who devoted their lives to providing spiritual comfort for Christian prisoners and the payment of ransoms from public charities in Europe. The Jewish business community was much involved also. Some acted as brokers, others as bankers who could advance monies in Barbary and obtain repayment in Europe through an associate or subsidiary bank. The Jews were particularly important because, being committed to neither the Christian nor the Mohammedan factions, they were acceptable to both. The Jews also trusted each other and could arrange large financial transactions by letter of credit all around the Mediterranean. Hence their deals were speedy and avoided the risks inherent in moving large sums of money from one country to another. For these services the brokers charged a commission of fifteen per cent plus interest on monies advanced. An additional life assurance service was available. If the temporary owner of a prisoner so wished he could insure that man's life, thus guaranteeing the return of his investment if the man died before any ransom was paid. The whole business was highly organised and the financial ramifications extended throughout all European and Mediterranean countries.

It was rare for a prisoner with a ransom on his head to remain in slavery for more than ten years. Those who served the longest periods, or who were simply re-sold abroad as life-time slaves, were the unfortunates who had no caring families to provide a ransom, or who had no skill to offer, or who came from a country

whose ruler was not disposed to pay tribute to the local Dey. There
were few who were not retrieved sooner or later, just as there were
very few who succeeded in escaping while awaiting release.

The situation regarding women prisoners was different. Having
no qualifications as craftsmen, labourers, or seamen, their future
was restricted to three possible avenues. If they were well
connected back home they might be ransomed quickly and then
released. Usually they were not physically molested, the Koran
being unequivocal on the subject of fornication and the treatment
of women. If pretty and intelligent they might be sought after as
wives for local men, either Christian or Muslim, wealthy enough to
afford them. If less desirable as formal wives, they could pass for
ever into the closed life of the harem where, as concubines, they
would suffer more than anything else from boredom and over-
eating. It is reported that they were encouraged to eat vast
quantities of bread soaked in syrup, there being a preference in
those days for ripeness in the female figure. Apart from the
wealthy, women prisoners in Barbary did not have an encouraging
prospect before them. It seems unlikely, however, that many of
them were deliberately tortured or maltreated. They were, like any
perishable commodity, too valuable to be damaged for spite or
sadistic pleasure. Quite certainly some of them were killed or
mutilated but, in general, it seems that this was punishment for
offences against the local criminal code or, in the case of apostates,
for breaches of Koranic teaching. These laws applied equally to
everyone in Barbary and each Dey would punish, with a severity
which to the European mind might seem excessive, any infraction

29

of those laws. To appear lax would invite the Dey's own rapid demise.

There are, however, many reports by former victims of the Corsairs which tell of sickening depravity and bestiality. Rape, murder, torture, mutilation, the accounts cover the full gamut of man's inhumanity to man. There can be no doubt that a certain proportion is true. There are four factors to be taken into account when one studies these reports. First, the political implications: reports of cruelty may have been exaggerated by those who sought to provoke the European powers into retaliatory action. Secondly, the commercial factor: individual sufferings may have been given lurid colouring in order to make the published memoirs of ransomed slaves more saleable to an avid public. Thirdly, the social factor: the Algerines were perpetrating their cruelties during the period when Torquemada was burning heretics at the stake in Spain and when drawing and quartering was a common punishment in England. The Algerines had no monopoly in vicious and inhuman punishments. Fourthly, the Corsairs of Malta, sailing under the flag of the Knights of the Order of St John of Jerusalem, were currently practising robbery and enslavement on an even greater scale than the Algerines.

Given these considerations, it is prudent to treat the published accounts with a degree of caution and to set them in perspective. The weight of evidence suggests that it was largely a matter of luck whether a prisoner was simply treated as an inanimate item of

merchandise or whether he was singled out for vicious torture. Algiers was not a stable country, it did not follow consistent policies. The behaviour of its people varied from year to year, even from day to day, according to the character of the incumbent Dey and his personal whims.

The instability of Algiers relates to the method by which the Deys rose to power. The republic maintained a fighting force of professional fighting men, the Janissaries. This elite group, numbering several thousand, controlled all aspects of Algerine society. Theirs was a privileged life, with excellent opportunities for advancement. Those who joined came from many backgrounds but even the most impoverished young man could look forward to acquiring considerable wealth, partly from his pay but mainly from his share of the profits made from privateering. He was allowed to have his own business interests and, if he possessed a particular skill, he could maintain a dual role of fighting soldier and merchant or craftsman. Not all of the Janissaries were Turks. Many had been Christians prior to capture by Corsair raiders. These were apostates, men who voluntarily renounced their original faith and embraced Islam. Other apostates had fled from Europe or from European ships, seeking refuge from prosecution for their crimes or from persecution for their beliefs. Their ranks were endowed with men of many talents and speaking many tongues. They included not only soldiers but also sailors, artisans, scholars, and adventurers of every kind. By virtue of being Janissaries, they were allowed to practice only the most casual observation of the Islamic laws. Although nominally Mohammedan, they were permitted tobacco, alcohol and opium. They led a pampered existence, having their own slaves and harems. In return they met three responsibilities: to garrison the towns, to police the hinterland, and to fight at sea during Corsair cruises.

The Janissaries elected from within their own ranks the man who would be the head of the state. The election was, in theory, by majority vote. However, the leader, entitled Dey or Bey, usually came from within the senior council of the Janissaries, known as the Divan. The Dey was a man of high repute among his fellow-Janissaries, wealthy enough to purchase the affection of his supporters, experienced in state-craft and administration but,

An 18th century view of Algiers. The unique symmetrical outline of the city was familiar to seafarers (National Maritime Museum)

most important of all, possessing enough cunning and instinct to stay alive. The story of the Barbary states is one of continuing power struggles. Palace revolts, disputes between different factions, divisions within ruling families, all led to eventual murder and armed conflict.

The richest, most ruthless and least democratic Dey was the one who stayed alive longest. It was not a post from which he could easily resign. A Dey was either in control or he was dead. The exception to this rule was to be found in Tripoli where, in 1711, a remarkable family dynasty was founded by Ahmed Karamanli. This family succeeded in retaining power for one hundred and twenty-five years in the teeth of constant pressure from within its own membership, from local opponents and from various other states. Algiers and Tunis never produced an equivalent dynasty. Sooner or later a Dey would be slain or, if he was lucky enough to die of natural causes, his chosen successor would be swept away in a welter of intrigue and blood-letting. This was most particularly the case in Algiers where, according to some eighteenth century commentators, the situation declined into 'near anarchy'.

Despite this anarchy, the European powers continued the same ambivalent policy towards the Algerines which they had displayed over several centuries. At first glance the situation was absurd. Here was a small ramshackle state, lacking any powerful ally, practising an alien religion, preying upon the merchant fleets of the world and earning its living by robbery and kidnap. Why did the Europeans not combine to deal a single crushing blow, wiping out this nest of Corsairs for ever? It was not such a simple proposition.

PRESA DELLA
GALEA DI SIMAIN
RAIS CORSARO

CHAPTER TWO

Wilberforce, Smith & the Americans

BETWEEN 1541 and 1829, Algiers was the target for eighteen separate military or naval expeditions by the Christian powers (see Appendix 1). All but the last failed to achieve an enduring solution to the problem. Time and again the Algerines were bombarded from the sea, devastated by earthquakes or weakened by epidemics of plague. On each occasion they recovered and returned to their old ways. On the face of it, they possessed a superhuman ability to overcome everything which nature and their enemies might throw at them. In practice, they were permitted to survive by virtue of the incompetence and the cynicism of those who otherwise should have ensured their destruction.

There is no doubt that any adventure against Algiers presented great difficulties. The North African coast is rocky and dangerous, swept by powerful currents and exposed to sudden violent storms. The ships of that period could not safely navigate the Mediterranean between November and March. The Europeans were frequently too busy fighting each other to have spare resources of men and ships for a major offensive against a distant and well-defended fortress like Algiers. In short, it was a tough nut to crack and the Christians lacked adequate tools for the job.

That said, however, there was a lack of political will. Despite the depredations of the Corsairs, each European power stood to gain in some way, from time to time, by maintaining a fragile friendship with the Algerine Deys. In the case of England, for example, there was a strong religious consideration. Following Henry VIII's break with Rome, there was a powerful national sentiment against Spain and the Inquisition. From the reign of King James II the popular cry was 'No Popery here!'. The Moors were the sworn enemies of Spain, having been driven from Granada and Sicily, and were therefore to a degree the allies of England in countering the influence of the Spaniards and the Roman Catholic church. In 1686 the city of Buda (present-day Budapest, capital of Hungary) was recaptured from the Turks by a Christian army under the Duke of Lorraine. When the news reached London the Spanish Ambassador to the Court of St James, Don Pedro Ronquillo, decorated his house in celebration. This aroused the fury of the mob who broke all his windows. Order was restored only after the Foot Guards and the Life Guards had been called out. The general opinion was that it would have been better if Buda had remained in Turkish hands rather than be taken by the Roman Catholics. Against this background England was content to tread warily in her dealings with Barbary.

She embarked upon a policy of negotiating a series of treaties. This was done by sending merchantmen into the Mediterranean in convoy, and escorted by warships. The Corsairs could achieve little against this type of force. An understanding was therefore reached whereby the Corsairs would refrain from attacking English merchantmen, or taking English slaves, while in return the Barbary states would receive from England a regular tribute to compensate for their loss of earnings. The tribute was paid partly in currency and goods, and partly in the form of cannon, firearms, powder and ship-building materials.

The other major European powers entered into similar treaties, Sweden, Holland, Spain and France all making substantial gifts of money and munitions of war to obtain protection for their maritime trade. To some extent these gifts were counter-productive because the treaties were frequently suspended or ignored and European ships would then find themselves threatened by weapons supplied originally by their own country. Furthermore, powerful batteries covering the Barbary ports became ever more imposing as they were strengthened with cannon supplied from all over Europe. On balance, the Europeans felt that it was easier and cheaper to live with the system of treaties, humiliating and inconvenient as it was at times, rather than engage in a bloody and expensive war.

This attitude continued for many decades, long after the Reformation, long after the retreat of the Holy Roman Empire and long after the navies of northern Europe had achieved the capacity to mount powerful long-range punitive expeditions. Access to the Barbary coast offered certain advantages. For example, during the Revolutionary and Napoleonic Wars (1793 - 1815), Great Britain frequently found herself fighting alone against France and her satellites. Sorely in need of even the most unlikely allies, the British were glad to make use of the port facilities of Barbary. Wellington's troops in the Peninsula were fed with grain and beef bought in Tetuan, Tunis and Algiers. Ships of the Royal Navy, perhaps battered by storm or cannon-fire, could seek temporary refuge in the Corsair havens. It made good sense to maintain a temporary superficial friendship with the Deys.

Apart from religious and military considerations, there was also a moral factor involved. Early in the eighteenth century the humanitarian movement had become evident in European philosophy. The Christian teaching that 'all men are born equal' became a socio-philosophical creed. The ideas of Rousseau and his contemporaries created the climate in which the American and French revolutions germinated and developed. The same ideas brought about the campaign against black slavery, the Abolitionist movement. In England, men such as Wilberforce, Sharp, Ramsay, Buxton and Paine devoted much of their lives to mobilising public opinion, while in America the Quakers played a similar role. Year after year, passions ran high and debate on the subject continued at fever pitch. Abolition of the slave trade, the traffic in human lives from Africa to the Americas, was a dominating issue as the nineteenth century opened.

It is a curious fact that the Abolitionists directed their efforts exclusively at the *black* slave trade. One can find no evidence that these brilliant and dedicated men ever uttered a single criticism of the enslavement of Muslims by the Christian Corsairs of Malta, or the enslavement of Christians by the Muslim Corsairs of Barbary. It is strange that this should be so for they cannot have been unaware of the facts. Certainly in the case of Algiers, the facts had been known and widely publicised throughout Europe since the sixteenth century. The Royal Navy was particularly well informed on the subject, and some senior officers resented deeply the persistent warfare waged by the Corsairs against legitimate merchant shipping. Nelson, for example, took it as a slight upon Great Britain's honour that the raiders should go unpunished. In 1799 he wrote, 'My blood boils that I cannot chastise these pirates. They could not show themselves in the Mediterranean did not our

country permit. Never let us talk of the cruelty of the African slave trade while we permit such a horrid war'.

As a serving officer there was little that Nelson could do to influence either international opinion or his own government's policy, especially in time of war with France. The responsibility of arousing public sentiment remained for many years in the hands of the Abolitionists and they recognised only one colour, black. Perhaps they believed in a policy of gradual progress: first destroy black slavery and then it would be so much easier to end Christian enslavement.

Nelson was again involved with Algerine affairs in 1804 while commanding the Mediterranean fleet. The British Consul, Falcon, had been deported by the Dey following a trumped-up charge of having kept his own harem of Moorish women in the Consulate. Nelson sent one of his senior officers to Algiers to protest at this insult to Great Britain, and also sought orders from London regarding possible punitive action. The affair, in fact, soon blew over and Nelson was obliged to shelve his plans, although he disliked the situation intensely. He wanted either to bombard the place or to impose an economic blockade. Algiers was particularly vulnerable to a full naval blockade because the population was dependent upon sea trade and the economy required a steady inflow of ransom and tribute, but strangely this tactic was never tried by any of Algiers' enemies. Certainly it would have been impossible in Nelson's time, the Royal Navy being committed heavily to the blockade of France and her European satellites.

One man more than any other mobilised influential opinion against the Deys of Algiers. He was Admiral Sir William Sidney Smith, a brilliant and controversial retired naval officer. His career began when he joined the Royal Navy in 1777 at the age of twelve, being appointed midshipman in HMS *Tortoise* under Viscount Howe. His subsequent adventures included a daring attempt to burn the French fleet in Toulon harbour, service against Russia under the King of Sweden, an escape from a Paris prison, and an inspired defence of Acre which frustrated Napoleon's plans for the conquest of central Asia and India. His service in Morocco, Egypt and the Levant as a naval officer, together with his diplomatic experience as Joint Minister Plenipotentiary at the Sublime Porte (Constantinople, Court of the Ottomans), had given him an unusually detailed knowledge and understanding of the Turk mentality. Sidney Smith was also a humanitarian. He had witnessed much of the suffering caused by the enslavement of Christians. He detested certain Turkish practices but, paradoxically, admired many of the Turk's qualities of character. Similarly, he fought for years against the France of Napoleon's regime but was nevertheless devoted to the French nation, taking up residence in Normandy before the war and retiring in Paris at the end of his career. As a consequence Smith was uniquely situated: he had the reputation, the experience, the detailed awareness and the international connections required to mobilise European opinion.

He made his first move in 1814 by founding an organisation which he named 'The Knights Liberator of the Slaves in Africa' and of which he appointed himself President. Frustrated in his attempts to continue a naval career and disappointed at the lack of recognition by the British government of his past services, he devoted all his time and much of his personal fortune to launching a massive exercise in public relations. Single-handed he started a campaign to arouse international action by writing to the heads of every state in Europe, to men of letters, to political leaders and to various potentates in Africa. Within months he had received several thousand letters in reply, all pledging support. Among them was a surprisingly warm and cordial response from Lord Exmouth.

Admiral Smith's last sea-going appointment before retirement had been as second-in-command to Exmouth, then Sir Edward Pellew, in the Mediterranean. The two men were of widely differing temperaments. Exmouth expressed a considerable dislike for his subordinate. Now, in 1814, he accepted Smith's invitation to become a Knight Liberator and wrote: ' . . . I had read with much interest your address to the sovereigns of Europe and I believe the feeling of interest it has created is general . . . I am greatly obliged to you, my dear Sir Sidney, for thinking of me among your knights . . . I shall give it all the support I can'. Here is firm evidence that, two years before the battle of Algiers, Lord Exmouth was committed morally and emotionally to the destruction of that city's regime. Less reliable evidence exists in the form of a rumour which claimed that a member of the Pellew family had been held captive for twenty-four years in North Africa in the early eighteenth century.

Smith wrote also to William Wilberforce, inviting the old man's support and collaboration. No doubt he hoped to benefit from the Abolitionist's established reputation and political experience, but Wilberforce's reply was cool, almost disdainful. It became clear that Smith's campaign to free the Christian slaves would be starting from scratch: it would receive no advantage from the momentum already created by the anti-black slavery campaigners. At this distance in time it is difficult to understand the mentality of Wilberforce and his colleagues. Perhaps, having battled against great difficulties for many years, they were simply jealous of Smith's rapid and dramatic entry onto the anti-slavery stage.

Smith succeeded in holding the first meeting of his 'Knights Liberator' in Vienna in September, 1814, during the meeting of Congress which was deciding the future of Europe. The Congress passed a resolution condemning all forms of slavery, but it did not specify how it was to be ended. Smith's major work, widely read and entitled *Mémoire sur la necessité et les moyens de faire cesser les Pirateries des Etats Barbaresque* was published on October 14, 1814, in Paris and Turin.

In 1815 his efforts were interrupted by Napoleon's dramatic escape from Elba. On the eve of Waterloo the Admiral happened to be making a private visit to Brussels with his wife. Eager and impulsive as ever and sensing that a great and decisive battle was about to take place, the old warrior organised an ambulance convoy of waggons hired at his own expense and attached himself to Wellington's army. The first noncombatant to congratulate the Duke after his victory, Smith spent the next three days supervising the rescue of wounded soldiers who had been left for dead on the field of battle. One hundred and thirty-four men, the majority Frenchmen and Prussians, were saved from the callous attentions of the scavenging Belgian peasants.

Returning to his Paris home, the little Admiral resumed his bombardment of letters on the subject of Christian slavery. Lord Castlereagh, the British Foreign Secretary, had come under strong pressure at Vienna to stop preaching on the subject and, instead, to start taking practical action. Nothing could be done immediately; it would be extremely hazardous to despatch a squadron to the Barbary coast during the winter months. However, at the first opportunity, in March of 1816, Admiral Lord Exmouth made his first visits to the three Deys (at Tripoli, Tunis and Algiers). The die was cast. Historically it was logical that, sooner or later, Algiers would be the target for a smashing blow such as that to be delivered by Exmouth in August. For this, the solo efforts of Admiral Sir William Sidney Smith must be recognised as the essential catalyst.

There was one other important ingredient in the story of Lord Exmouth's bombardment of Algiers. It concerns the early history of the United States Navy and, to understand the interaction between the two, it is necessary to examine the events of the preceding twenty years.

Prior to the War of Independence, the colonists of North America did not possess a navy of their own. Their merchant ships enjoyed the protection of the Royal Navy, officially at least. In practice they, too, had suffered substantial loss at the hands of the Barbary Corsairs, mainly in the Atlantic and the Western

Approaches. With the outbreak of hostilities between Great Britain and America in 1775, there was an immediate need by the thirteen colonies for a naval force. Their fledgling navy played a useful part in the revolution, particularly on the great inland waterways and lakes.

The declarations of war upon Great Britain, by France in 1778, by Spain in 1779, and by the Netherlands in 1780, spread the resources of the Royal Navy very thinly indeed. The American ships were therefore not pressed as hard as they might otherwise have been. On land, after much tough campaigning, the British Army was beaten and forced to surrender at Yorktown in 1781. The war ended with the Treaty of Paris in 1783, and the

The squadron commanded by Commodore William Bainbridge USN returns in triumph from the Barbary Coast in 1815. The leading ship is the USS Independence (US Naval Academy Museum, Annapolis)

41

independence of the United States was formally recognised. The Congress now decided that a navy was no longer required and it was disbanded.

The return of peace was followed by an expansion in international trade. American merchant ships started to visit the Mediterranean and the western seaboard of Europe with growing frequency. But having no navy to protect them, they soon fell prey to the Corsairs and again their losses soared.

Congress reacted by passing legislation in 1794 which re-established the navy. Resolutions of this nature can be approved of course, far more quickly that they can be put into operation: it takes time to create major shipyards, to assemble a skilled work-force, to recruit a body of seamen and officers, and to work up to the level of efficiency required for distant-water duty. In fact the new navy received its baptism of fire not against the Corsairs but in the undeclared war with France in 1799-1800.

Meanwhile, American diplomats were negotiating for the ransom of enslaved United States citizens. The captors explained the niceties of the long-established system, suggesting that America too would find it expedient to pay regular tribute in the form of money, weapons, powder and shot. The tribute or gift would undoubtedly facilitate diplomatic relations and quite possibly lead to a reduction in the number of merchantmen seized

by Corsair raiders. So argued the Deys, with the added advice that
America would be well advised to follow the example set by the
Christian states of Europe. As might be expected of a vigorous
young nation which had just emerged triumphant from a war of
independence with one of the most powerful nations on earth, the
United States reacted aggressively to this line of reasoning.
Thomas Jefferson had been elected President and he thundered his
country's view, 'millions for defence, not one cent for tribute'. He
started to despatch strong squadrons of fighting ships to the
Mediterranean and these were rotated frequently. For two years
the Americans tried the old established formula of talking softly
and carrying a big stick, but they soon tired of the duplicity of the
Barbary Deys. In 1803 they began an all-out war, their efforts
directed by Commodore Edward Preble.

By 1805 the Regency of Tripoli had been forced into making a
lasting peace with America and had returned her slaves. This
campaign was illuminated by some wonderfully brave and
thrilling adventures, one of the most extraordinary being an
attempt to attack Tripoli with a military force which marched
across the desert from Egypt. This force included a detachment of
United States Marines and the event is commemorated in the
battle hymn of the Corps, 'from the Halls of Montezuma to the
shores of Tripolee'.

Despite their objections in principle, the Americans continued
to pay tribute to Tunis and Algiers. Their navy was unable to give
its undivided attention to attempting an armed suppression of
these states, being diverted by another campaign against the Royal
Navy, the War of 1812, from which it emerged covered with glory.
The British suffered a reverse in the one sphere where they had
considered themselves supreme, the exercise of maritime power.

In 1814 the Americans decided once and for all to impose a
settlement with Tunis and Algiers. As soon as the next cruising
season opened in 1815, they despatched a squadron to the
Mediterranean under the command of Commodore Stephen
Decatur. He first visited Tunis, where he negotiated successfully

with the Dey, obtaining a payment of $46,000 as compensation for earlier violations of the treaty between the two countries. He then sailed on to Tripoli, gaining further payment and the release of some Danish and Neapolitan slaves.

Decatur's squadron was now relieved by five large frigates, commanded by Commodore William Bainbridge, arriving direct from America. His first port of call was Tripoli where he found the Dey in a compliant mood, having been thoroughly over-awed by Decatur's visit a few weeks earlier. Bainbridge then sailed on to Tunis where again he found the local leader anxious to maintain a friendly relationship with the United States. In both instances the American was given firm assurances that his nation's shipping would never again be molested.

Decatur's squadron now returned to the Barbary Coast, having made a diplomatic and provisioning visit to Messina, and steered into the bay of Algiers. The Commodore was carrying a personal message from the President, James Madison, to the new Dey, Omar Bashaw. The terms of Madison's letter were unequivocal: the United States firmly intended to pay no more tribute; they required the immediate release of all their citizens currently held in captivity, the release of all ships and cargoes taken from them by the Corsairs, and the restitution of part of the previous cash payments made to the Algerines. Failing an immediate agreement — and Decatur gave the Dey only three hours in which to decide — the United States would take whatever action it thought necessary.

There was nothing novel about the American proposals; many other naval officers had sailed into Algiers in former decades bearing similar letters. On this occasion the essential difference was the immense reputation which the United States Navy had earned for itself in the War of 1812. If there was one thing which the Algerines respected it was the successful application of armed force. They were acutely aware of the fact that they were now dealing with a navy which had trounced the previously all-conquering Royal Navy. Contemporary reports of the meetings held in Algiers in June, 1815, make it plain that the Algerines were profoundly anxious to placate the United States. With little discussion, they agreed all the main articles of the proposed peace treaty and it was signed on behalf of the President by Commodore Decatur and by William Shaler, the United States Consul at Algiers.

Two of the heroes of the American campaign against the Barbary states.
Commodore William Bainbridge USN (left) and Commodore Stephen
Decatur USN (right). Their successes provoked jealousy and resentment in
England, but many Royal Navy officers grudgingly admired Bainbridge's
conduct during the war of 1812. In December of that year, while commanding
the USS Constitution, he destroyed HMS Java in a ship-to-ship duel.
Bainbridge's chivalry and personal kindness towards his defeated British
opponents was a feature of the episode (Royal Naval Museum)

Decatur and Bainbridge returned to a hero's welcome in
America. They had gained everything they had set out to achieve.
This was one of the few occasions when the Algerines made a
promise and kept it. American shipping, after 1815, was given free
passage by the Corsairs.

It is not difficult to imagine the reaction to all this in England.
The Americans were far from popular, particularly at the
Admiralty. The Royal Navy was not accustomed to being
outshone, certainly not by a smaller adversary which lacked a great
sea-faring tradition, and the resentment ran deep. It was bad
enough that Decatur and Bainbridge should have been able to
frighten the Dey into submission, without a shot having been
fired, but it was intolerable that they should have done so at a time

when so many British subjects were still languishing in Algerine *bagnios*. To rub salt in the wound, Decatur chose to sail his squadron into the harbour of Britain's bastion, Gibraltar, on the pretext of passing a signal to an American sloop of war anchored there, the USS *Ontario*. His ships sailed in as though for a yachting review, giving an admirable exhibition of ship handling, and then tacked out to sea again without dropping anchor. The crowds of British officers and citizens who gathered to watch were impressed by the professional skill of this display but were not amused by the impudent spirit which prompted it.

And so we have a number of powerful human emotions starting to combine and create an explosive mixture. For years the British had been frustrated by the cavalier treatment handed out to them by the Algerines. For the past two years they had smarted under the memory of their defeats during the War of 1812. For the past year they had been under pressure from the resolutions passed at the Congress of Vienna. Now there was the additional factor of jealousy and resentment generated by the brilliant American coup. In the individual case of Lord Exmouth himself, there was the question of his personal honour: he had declared his loyalty to Sir Sidney Smith's 'Knights Liberator' and had pledged his active support. There is no record of Exmouth's own attitude toward the Americans but it is fair to assume that he was no more fond of them than any other senior officer of the Royal Navy (particularly as they had killed his young brother John in the fighting at Saratoga).

History might have taken a very different course if there had not existed such a deep animosity between the two English-speaking navies. For example, Britain's Mediterranean fleet could have combined with the two squadrons led by Decatur and Bainbridge when they visited Algiers in 1815. Britain's peace treaty with the Dey might then have been as advantageous as that signed by Decatur and Shaler. Alternatively, if the United States Navy had been defeated in the War of 1812, and if the Royal Navy's reputation had remained supreme, then perhaps it would have been the Americans who would have been obliged to resort to armed force against Algiers. The roles adopted by the two countries could have been so easily reversed. In the event it was the outcome of the earlier encounters between the two navies and the emotional interplay between the two nations which predestined, in part at least, the violence of the attack by Lord Exmouth.

CHAPTER THREE

The Turk & the Cornishman

THE BOMBARDMENT OF ALGIERS in 1816 was the result of a complicated cross-current of issues and animosities extending over many decades. However, the final steps leading to the battle were taken by the two opposing leaders, Admiral Lord Exmouth and the Dey of Algiers. The events of that year were heavily influenced by the personalities of these two men and the manner in which they reacted to each other. History has left us with a detailed knowledge of one, a much sketchier picture of the other.

The Dey of Algiers had been in power less than twelve months when he and Exmouth had their first encounter. His name was Omar Bashaw, although he appears in various accounts of the battle under different guises: Omar Pashaw, Omar bin Mohammed, and Osman Pasha. Forty-two years of age, of medium build, olive-skinned and with keen flashing eyes, he impressed his visitors as an alert and intelligent leader. His mother tongue was Turkish and he had a good grasp of colloquial Arabic and French, but he was illiterate in all three. He had no formal education, his arrival at the peak of power being attributed to basic ruthlessness and native wit rather than intellectual ability. A former Janissary, he had risen to be Agha or leader of that elite before being elected Dey on April 7, 1815. His predecessor had ruled for only sixteen days before being slowly strangled to death in public by his own soldiers.

Omar Bashaw remained in total command of his people throughout the events of 1816 and was not seriously challenged by any of his rivals. He was without doubt a tough and worthy opponent.

We have a far more detailed record of the career of Lord

Exmouth. He was born in Dover on April 19, 1757. One of six children, he grew up in comfortable surroundings, his father being employed as a captain with the Dover Packet Service. When his father died the family returned to Penzance where the children were brought up by relatives.

Educated at Truro Grammar School, he entered the Royal Navy in December, 1770, almost the same date as another unknown little boy began his service, Horatio Nelson. Edward had barely reached thirteen years of age when he was appointed captain's servant to Captain Stott, commanding HMS *Juno*.

Stott made an uneventful cruise to the Falklands and then assumed command of HMS *Alarm*, a 32-gun frigate. Edward Pellew followed his captain into this ship with the rank of midshipman. For the next three years they served with the Mediterranean Fleet and Pellew was promoted master's mate. The only episode of interest during this time was a visit by HMS *Alarm* to Algiers during one of the interminable squabbles between that country and Great Britain. Captain Stott delivered a formal complaint to the Dey regarding the maltreatment of the British Consul. The Algerine rejected Stott's submission and obliged him to remove the Consul from the country. It was part of a depressing pattern of events.

Young Pellew's service in HMS *Alarm* ended abruptly in 1775 when a mild prank irritated Captain Stott so much that he sacked the boy, putting him ashore at Marseilles. Returning to England he secured a posting as able seaman in the 36-gun frigate, HMS *Blonde*, commanded by Captain Philemon Pownall. Pellew's career now entered a new and vital stage. As soon as she was ready for sea HMS *Blonde* sailed for Canada in company with HMS *Juno* and twenty transports. The convoy was bearing General Burgoyne and the army which was destined to meet its fate at Saratoga.

With the arrival of the expedition in the St Lawrence, and the defeat of the American attempt to seize the city of Quebec, the scene of action moved south to Lake Champlain and here Edward Pellew had his first opportunity to distinguish himself. The Americans had a small fleet of warships operating on the lake; the British had none. The lake was the only gateway between Quebec and the River Hudson, in what today is upper New York State. The British built a small fleet of fighting ships on the lake shore with which to destroy the American vessels and so open the way to New York. Pellew was sent south with a detachment of twenty men to assist with the construction and manning of these vessels. He was restored to the rank of midshipman and appointed mate, or third in command, of the newly-completed armed schooner *Carleton*. In their first engagement his captain and the master's mate quickly became casualties so, at the age of nineteen, Pellew found himself commanding a warship, hard hit and under heavy fire. He acquitted himself well, showed complete disregard for personal danger and was noted by various senior officers as being an outstanding young man. His services were brought to the attention of Lord Howe and Lord Sandwich and he was confirmed in his command of *Carleton*. He remained on Lake Champlain for the next few months, a happy young man with his own small ship and free of any immediate supervision.

The following Spring brought a renewal of the British drive southwards. Pellew was attached to the army with a small body of seamen, his task being that of trying to gain the use of the upper reaches of the Hudson as a supply-line. He mobilised a small flotilla of barges and, by his personal ingenuity and bravery, was able to sustain the army for a while. Eventually the weather, combined with lack of food, forced the British into surrender and General 'Gentleman Johnny' Burgoyne selected Pellew to carry his despatch back to London thus allowing him to avoid captivity. The despatch included a warm tribute to Pellew's activities and he was confirmed in his promotion to the rank of lieutenant.

There followed two years of routine duties at Spithead and off Newfoundland before he found himself again serving under Captain Pownall, now commanding HMS *Apollo*. They sailed from Plymouth and were soon involved in three lively actions with French ships. The third of these was a fight with a large frigate off the coast near Ostend and Pownall was killed by a cannon-ball in the early part of the engagement. Pellew assumed command and forced the French ship into shoal water where she stranded. Pellew had again showed courage and initiative and he received a letter of congratulation from Lord Sandwich, First Lord of the Admiralty.

During the next two years he commanded small sloops of war on the east and south coasts of England, acting as a deterrent to smugglers and French privateers. In May of 1782 he was promoted to the rank of post-captain, the most important step in a naval officer's career. He was only twenty-five years of age. However, within a few months the American War of Independence ended

Captain Philemon Pownall RN, was one of the ablest captains of his day, and also one of the wealthiest. In 1762, when commanding the sloop Favourite, he had captured off Cadiz a Spanish treasure ship, the Hermione, inward bound from Lima with a cargo of silver. Pownall's share of the prize money was £64,872. His guide and mentor was Admiral Boscawen, under whom he had at one time served. Boscawen's brother was Lord Falmouth, friend of the Pellew family and young Edward's patron. The two older men persuaded Pownall to take this promising youngster under his wing. In an age when patronage was no less important than ability, it was a vital move. Pownall was highly intelligent, a strict disciplinarian and an innovator. He agreed to accept the lad on condition that he started from the bottom rung of the ladder (dropping rank from master's mate to able seaman). Despite his premature death, Pownall was able to develop Edward Pellew's inherent talents and to teach him the ways of leadership. Without that influence Pellew might never have risen to assume the command at Algiers (photo by Sothebys)

and the greater part of the Royal Navy was laid up. Pellew spent the next three years ashore, unemployed and on half pay.

Early in 1786 he was appointed to command HMS *Winchelsea,* 32 guns, for service on the Newfoundland station. For four years he served in the North Atlantic on routine peace-time duties, growing in reputation as an outstanding seaman and as a hard disciplinarian. Relatively minor offences by members of his crew earned them as many as four dozen lashes. For a time he commanded HMS *Salisbury,* the 50-gun flagship of the Newfoundland squadron, and then settled down for a year to work the family farm at Treverry, near Falmouth. By all accounts he was a poor farmer.

Pellew was rescued from Treverry by the declaration of war with France in February, 1793. He was given command of a 40-gun frigate, HMS *Nymphe,* a beautiful ship which was well armed but lacked rigging, spars and crew. The press gangs of Portsmouth had already swept up every available seaman in the area which meant that Pellew had to scrape together a mixed body of landsmen to train. Eighty of these were Cornish tin-miners who had never previously been to sea. Pellew's only valuable acquisition was a man named John Gaze, mate of a small merchant ship, *Venus*, whom he persuaded to transfer, with a bounty of £5, to the King's service. Pellew now had an experienced watch-keeping officer who, despite his youth (Gaze was 21) and his lack of combat experience, could assist him in the urgent task of readying the ship for war. They did not know it at the time, but both Pellew and Gaze had just taken an important step in their lives. They were to serve together for most of their naval careers; they were to become lasting friends and Gaze would eventually become Pellew's fleet navigator and sailing master (Master of the Fleet).

Next came the episode which was to transform Edward Pellew from a promising young post-captain into a figure of national prominence. On June 19, 1793, he was cruising in *Nymphe* off Start Point, South Devon, on passage from Falmouth to Portsmouth, when he sighted the French frigate *La Cléopatre,* a ship of equal force to his own. Each captain was eager to fight and they closed rapidly, the crews each giving three cheers and the two commanding officers raising their hats in gestures of courtesy. This was the first time in the present war that major units from each navy had met in single combat and they charged at each other like knights on the field of chivalry.

After a furious cannonade, with heavy casualties on both sides, the French were finally beaten into submission. 'We dished her up in fifty minutes', Pellew later wrote to his brother Samuel. He boarded *La Cléopatre,* comforted her dying captain, and then brought her into Portsmouth as prize. It was a tremendous boost to British morale and Pellew received an ecstatic welcome. King George III himself announced the victory from his box at the Covent Garden opera house and he honoured Pellew with a knighthood. Other officers were rewarded with honours and promotions. One of the rewards went to Pellew's brother, Israel, serving in HMS *Nymphe* as a supernumary.

Pellew then succeeded to the command of a larger and better armed ship, the frigate HMS *Arethusa,* his new base was Falmouth, and he moved his household to the nearby village of Flushing. His area of operations was the Bay of Biscay and the Western Approaches. *Arethusa* formed part of a squadron of frigates under the command of Commodore Sir John Warren. In the language of a much later war, this was a hunter-killer group, its mission being to sweep clean the vital sea-lanes to the south-west of the British Isles.

Two important actions soon followed in both of which Sir Edward Pellew distinguished himself. The first was a battle near Guernsey where he took the French frigate *La Pomone* as prize, and the second came a few months later when he captured another big frigate, the *Revolutionnaire*. Both prizes were bought into the service of the Royal Navy and Pellew's personal fortune started to grow. His good name at the Admiralty was recognised when he was given command of the Falmouth squadron in place of Warren.

Then an episode occurred which made Pellew a folk-hero in the West Country. On January 26, a strong south westerly gale was blowing into Plymouth Sound. One of the many ships sheltering there was the *Dutton*, a transport hired by the War Office for the movement of troops to the West Indies. On board she had a large number of soldiers, many sick with fever. The Master tried to send these ashore but small boats were unable to operate in the turbulent waters of the Sound. It was decided to sail the *Dutton* to a sheltered inlet known as the Cattewater. The *Dutton* started to make the move, struck a reef under Mountbatten Cliff, lost her rudder and was quickly swept onto the rocks under the Citadel. The impact immediately brought down all her masts and huge waves burst over her stern. The

The encounter which propelled a promising young post captain to over-night fame and earned him a knighthood; the fight off Start Point between HMS Nymphe and the French frigate La Cléopatré

decks were jammed with four hundred soldiers and nearly a hundred seamen and civilian passengers who were in extreme peril. A large crowd collected on the cliffs and along the Hoe to watch the spectacle.

Pellew heard news of the wreck as he arrived with Lady Pellew to dine with friends in Plymouth. He reacted by running to the shore and had himself hauled out to the ship by life-line. Once aboard he found total terror and panic, many of the men being helplessly drunk after breaking into the ship's rum store. He laid about them with the flat of his sword and was able to restore order. A number of small boats battled their way out to the *Dutton* from the Barbican, and Pellew supervised the loading of these with the sick and the women and children. He stayed aboard most of the day until practically everyone was ashore. The merchantman continued to pound hard on the rocks and she finally disintegrated as the last of her passengers was rescued.

His enterprise and personal courage were rewarded with a Baronetcy and he became Sir Edward Pellew, Bart, of Treverry. He rented a fine house in Falmouth and settled to enjoy his public fame and professional reputation. Not yet forty, he had risen far and fast, he was happily married with four children, and commanded an elite squadron operating from his home town. It was the happiest time of his career.

In 1796 Pellew became involved in two rebellions. The first was an attempt by the British to land arms and stores in Western France where the Catholic population, under Royalist leadership, was in armed revolt against the atheist revolutionary regime in Paris. The rebels, known as Chouans, dominated the Brest peninsula and threatened the vital naval base of that name. A first attempt by the British to assist the rebels had failed miserably a year earlier at Quiberon Bay, and Pellew's task now was to breathe fresh life into the Chouan spirit of resistance. In the event he was unable to do so, but he did create havoc in the coastal shipping lanes and returned to Plymouth with two French frigate prizes which his squadron had captured.

The second affair was the attempt by France to land an army in Ireland. The Catholic Irish, not for the first or last time, were in open rebellion against the Protestant English. The French believed that they could seriously embarrass Great Britain by bringing aid to the Irish and to this end they assembled a large fleet at Brest. The troops on board amounted to eighteen

January 27, 1796: the shattered wreck of the Dutton stranded
under the cliffs of Plymouth Hoe, only the lonely figure of
Sir Edward Pellew remaining on her poop-deck

thousand men complete with artillery and horses. The fleet
slipped out of Brest harbour and got clear away from the
blockading British squadron. The French Admiral's intention
was to land at Bantry Bay but his orders stated that he was to
avoid battle with the Royal Navy during the passage. The first
night brought foul weather and heavy cloud. In the darkness the
French ships lost sight of each other and the fleet started to
disintegrate.

Pellew was in the area with his squadron of frigates and he even
came within gunshot of the French Commander-in-Chief's ship,
but in wild weather on a perilous lee shore, the two forces were
more concerned with avoiding shipwreck than with killing each
other. The French succeeded in getting most of their ships away
into deeper water and some days later they started to arrive in twos

and threes at Bantry Bay. The French Commander-in-Chief was one of the last to appear, and when he did he found that the first arrivals had already lost heart and had sailed back to Brest. The landing never took place and the whole adventure was a fiasco.

In the meanwhile, Pellew had raced back to Falmouth for orders. In England all was confusion and anger. The French were out and nobody knew where they had gone. Pellew was immediately given orders to cruise the Biscay coast and to seek information of the French intentions. He had his own theory, believing the French fleet had sailed for Lisbon. He searched as far south as Corunna but found nothing. Returning northwards he fell in with one of his own frigates, HMS *Amazon,* and together they sailed towards Brest. On January 13, 1797, they sighted and gave chase to a French warship, making the return passage from Bantry Bay. She was *Les Droits de L'Homme,* a 74-gun ship of the line with enough fire-power to blow a frigate to pieces with a single broadside if given the chance. Unfortunately for the French their ship was of an experimental design, being set low in the water, and it was discovered that her lower gun ports were unusuable owing to the rough state of the sea. However, she was carrying nearly eight hundred soldiers and they were lined up along both bulwarks where their muskets poured a hail of lead into the two British frigates which were snapping at her flanks.

For ten hours, through the darkening evening and on through the night, the three ships raced along parallel tracks, blazing away at each other whenever wind, sea and visibility gave them the opportunity. Shortly before dawn breakers were seen dead ahead: they had charged full bore into Audierne Bay, not far south of Brest. Pellew instantly broke off the action and, by brilliant ship handling and good luck, clawed his way out of the trap. For the *Amazon* and *Droits de L'Homme* it was too late, they ran aground, lost their masts and were pounded to pieces by the waves. The officers and crew of the *Amazon* were saved and became prisoners of the French, but most of the men in the *Droits de L'Homme* were drowned.

In 1799, after serving nearly thirty years exclusively in frigates, Pellew was appointed to command a ship of the line, HMS *Impetueux,* 74. He was bitterly angry when he received his orders. Accustomed all his service life to independent commands and freedom of action, he would now find himself lumbering around in company with the other major ships of the Channel Fleet and directly under the eye of an admiral whom he disliked intensely, Lord Bridport. Worse still, he knew that he was to have *Impetueux* for the sole reason that she was the problem child of Bridport's fleet. There was nothing wrong with the vessel herself but the ship's company was known to be on the point of mutiny. Any captain taking on such a task had everything to lose and nothing to gain. If his men mutinied their captain's career would be wrecked. On the other hand, there were no rewards for captains whose crews were restrained from open mutiny. Pellew protested long and loud to no avail and went aboard in March, 1799. Two months later the ratings fulfilled all expectations by refusing to take orders. Pellew arrested the ring-leaders, three were hanged and five were flogged around the fleet. Discipline was restored but the *Impetueux* was never a happy ship.

In 1800 he was again involved in attempts to discomfit the French by returning to the Biscay coast where he landed arms and stores for the few remaining bands of Chouans. Two even more ambitious projects involved the proposed capture of Belleisle (a sizeable island situated ten miles off the coast at Quiberon Bay) and a landing at Ferrol in northern Spain (where it was planned to destroy the naval base). On both occasions Pellew found himself in harness with army officers who lacked his own fiery determination. Both projects failed.

Returning to the endless treadmill of the blockade, *Impetueux* passed the following winter patrolling Brest and Rochefort until finally she paid off at Plymouth after the signing of theTreaty of Amiens (that uneasy declaration of peace between France and Great Britain which was to last little more than a year). The time Pellew had served in this ship was marred by frustration and disappointments and he and her sullen crew parted company with feelings of mutual relief in April, 1802.

Coming ashore in peacetime England, looking for something useful to occupy his time, Pellew fulfilled a long-felt ambition by standing as a candidate in the Parliamentary election. He was returned as joint member for Barnstaple in February, 1803. In London he spent most of his time visiting the Admiralty with the object of obtaining a new command and a few weeks later he was appointed to HMS *Tonnant*, 80, a fine ship taken from the French at the Battle of the Nile and fitting out at Plymouth. Pellew barely had time to make her ready for sea before war with France again broke out on May 16. He was sent south to watch the Spanish

Admiral Lord Exmouth after his return from Algiers. At his throat he wears the Grand Cross of a Knight of the Order of St Maurice and St Lazarus. On his breast and from his shoulder, the decorations and sashes of a Knight Grand Cross of the military division of the Order of the Bath and a Knight of the Order of St Ferdinand. The decorations, the gold braid and the thickened physique, all conceal the fact that in his prime he had been exceptionally strong and agile. Even in his forties, he could still climb to the cross-trees faster than many of his much younger officers (National Maritime Museum)

coast where he passed five tedious months blockading Ferrol before returning to England in February, 1804. He made his one and only appearance in the House of Commons and spoke brilliantly during an acrimonious debate regarding the conduct of the Admiralty and the deficiencies of the new ship-building programme. Having terminated his formal education at the age of twelve, and having spent the best part of three decades at sea, Pellew suddenly displayed a talent for oratory which surprised his contemporaries. This rough-hewn sailorman possessed an unexpected eloquence and sense of political awareness.

Promoted to Rear-Admiral of the White, Pellew was given command of the East Indies squadron and at the end of 1804 he sailed for India. The main British bases in the east were Bombay, Madras, Trincomalee and Penang. The French had a powerful force of cruisers in the Indian Ocean, based upon Mauritius, and they were taking an excessive toll of British merchant shipping.

Pellew's ships enjoyed a number of minor successes against French raiders during the next two years but nothing of great interest occurred until the end of 1806 when he launched an attack on the Dutch naval base at Batavia. In some ways this could be regarded as a minor dress rehearsal for the Battle of Algiers. The objective was a fleet anchorage and port installations protected by entrenched shore batteries. The sea approach was difficult, the waters being shallow and swept by strong currents. The Dutch did not put up a strong resistance, losing six small gun-boats and twenty merchantmen which were burned at their moorings. British losses were negligible. The British squadron was navigated by Gaze, still serving faithfully as Pellew's sailing master. Two of the smaller British vessels were commanded by Pellew's elder sons, Fleetwood and Pownall, who had enjoyed phenomenally rapid promotion in the Royal Navy as a result of their father's influence. Pellew had always indulged in the most blatant nepotism but, on this occasion at least, his fatherly trust was completely justified. The boys fought well and intelligently. Fleetwood Pellew was rewarded for this and other exploits by being given command of a 74-gun ship of the line, HMS *Powerful*, at the age of eighteen.

Sir Edward Pellew returned to England in 1809, newly promoted to the rank of vice-admiral, richer by £100,000 in prize money, but much reduced in health. He was now fifty-two years old.

Twelve months of rest and recuperation and he was scheming for a new command. He was successful, being appointed Commander-in-Chief, North Sea. This led to a dull and uneventful year of blockade work off Flushing and the Scheldt estuary before he received a more important post as Commander-in-Chief, Mediterranean, which meant taking over the task of blockading the French fleet in Toulon harbour.

At this time Pellew acquired a small estate to complement his social standing and as an investment for his sons. Lady Pellew concluded the purchase of Canonteign, ten miles south west of Exeter, and she also bought Bitton House in Teignmouth, on the South Devon coast, as a permanent family home.

Pellew remained in command of the powerful Mediterranean fleet from 1811 to 1814 when the Great War ended. Although he had as many as ninety ships under his orders in any single period, his resources were often stretched thinly. There was much to do: supporting the right flank of Wellington's campaign in the Peninsula, blockading Toulon, watching the Italian ports, and sustaining the Kingdom of the Two Sicilies. Adding to his problems was the arrival of Sir Sidney Smith as second-in-command: they did not work well together. Another arrival was Captain Fleetwood Pellew in command of the frigate *Resistance*. Fleetwood had inherited the worst of his father's temperament and he drove his men so hard that they mutinied. Ugly accounts of the affair reached London and, despite his father's intervention, the young man's career was effectively ruined.

The apparent return of peace, after twenty years of turmoil, led to an abundant distribution of honours and awards for the army and navy. Pellew was made a peer of the realm and granted a pension of £2,000 per annum. There was already a Lord Teignmouth so the name of another nearby seaport was chosen for his title and he became Lord Exmouth. By virtue of his seniority, he also became an Admiral of the Blue.

Admiral Lord Exmouth returned to England in August, 1814, and passed the winter with his family. In March of the following year he was re-appointed to command the Mediterranean fleet with HMS *Boyne*, 98, as his flagship. Napoleon had escaped from Elba and Europe was once again in uproar.

After some initial and comic-opera manoeuvrings at Naples, Lord Exmouth sailed for Genoa to embark an expeditionary force which he landed at Marseilles in support of a Royalist uprising. He went ashore with four thousand soldiers, sailors and marines and personally led them, on horseback, to seek battle. He cleared the surrounding area and went on to recapture Toulon. Despite his advancing years he had not lost his taste for freelance adventures.

With the final destruction of Napoleon's ambitions at Waterloo, it was natural for Exmouth to expect that he would be recalled and put out to grass. Instead he received orders to stay in the Mediterranean and to conclude new and lasting treaties with the three Barbary states. Apart from his one brief visit to Algiers forty years earlier, he had had no personal involvement with the Corsairs and their masters. However, like every other officer in the service, he was well aware of their reputation and the difficulties attaching to any attempt to suppress them.

It is appropriate at this point to summarise the picture which we have of Lord Exmouth. Professionally, he had a wide range of knowledge and experience. His time in Canada had taught him small boat construction, independent command, and combat with the Americans. The *Nymphe* which had served him so well off the coast of Devon in 1793 had taught him how to train a fighting crew from a motley crowd. Falmouth developed his taste for independent command. The *Dutton* had tested his personal physical courage. Saratoga, Brest, Belleisle and Ferrol were all unsuccessful land operations which involved collaboration with the army: they may have influenced his attitude towards the Algiers assault. On the other hand, Betavia and Marseilles proved his ability to organise effective assaults from the sea.

As a man, he was strong-willed, quick tempered, and inclined to petulance when baulked. Intensely loyal to his friends, he was excessively generous towards Cornishmen in general and his own relatives in particular. He was an open and forthright man, but fully capable of intriguing with and against diplomats and politicians. Customarily blunt of speech but capable of great eloquence when occasion demanded, he preferred independent action to team-work. A brilliant seaman and one of the Navy's few specialists in gunnery, he was not a particularly complex man and he possessed a number of characteristics which could with equal accuracy be used to describe a dozen other officers who had climbed to the top of their profession. In the case of Exmouth, however, there was something extra. Perhaps he was more intelligent, or cautious, or skilful, but whatever the explanation he was certainly more devoted to the concept of pre-battle planning than most of his contemporaries. Here was a precise and tidy mind teamed with a spirit which was always brave and intensely energetic. It was a formidable combination. Of all the admirals who had tangled with them, Lord Exmouth was the one whom the Algerines had most to fear. Omar Bashaw, still settling the reins of new-found power in his hands, had no idea what a thunderbolt was soon to strike his city.

CANONTEIGN HOUSE · CHRISTOW · SOUTH DEVON

CHAPTER FOUR

The opening moves

IN SEPTEMBER of 1815 secret orders reached Lord Exmouth from Whitehall. He was instructed to visit Tripoli, Tunis and Algiers and to arrange new peace treaties with each of the three Deys. We are not told how much freedom of action he was allowed in these orders, nor do we know the details of any negotiating weapons which the British government may have authorised him to employ. Looking back at the imprecise terms of reference given to many of Exmouth's predecessors, it is possible that he, too, was entering into this venture with nothing much more than pious hope to sustain him.

Immediate action was out of the question. The season of winter gales was about to start, thus precluding any possibility of an approach to the shores of North Africa by vessels larger than a frigate. No time was wasted, however, in laying plans well in advance. John Gaze went ashore at Marseilles to study the charts and mariners' notes held by the French cartographers. His investigations revealed the dismaying fact that large tracts of the Barbary coast had never been properly surveyed. Exmouth moved his squadron to Livorno (Leghorn) and settled in for the winter. At the first opportunity he detached a single ship, HMS *Banterer*, and sent her on a secret mission to reconnoitre the port of Algiers. This small frigate was to follow a roundabout route and have minimum contact with the shore.

The true purpose of her journey was to be known only to Lord Exmouth, his secretary and to the frigate's captain, Charles Warde. The written orders handed over by Exmouth to Captain Warde give a revealing insight into the workings of the Admiral's mind at this time:

Instructions to Captain Warde, on surveying Algiers

Leghorn, 25th January 1816

'Mem: — Endeavour to get the brig into the Mole, to do which, you must promise not to protect any slaves who may attempt to get on board.

The object of your mission is to discover with apparent indifference the state of Algiers, as to its defences both by land and sea, and the number of real troops they can depend on. The sea defences are the first object. If you are allowed to enter, endeavour to pass along the outside of the Mole, and sound the off-side of the brig, and so on until you anchor. Be precise in the distance of the Mole-head from the town, across, to ascertain if *Boyne* can place herself across the mouth of it.

Observe if she can be flanked, or raked from the walls, supposing her anchored with her head off sea-ward, and her stern to the city. Observe if any flanking batteries on either side can play upon her; particularly if the Lighthouse battery can fire in that direction down the Mole. Take notice if from the walls or houses, a ship so placed would be commanded by musketry. I believe the walls are high: take minutes of the number of guns mounted on the sea-face of the Mole and Light-house, and if of heavy calibre. Minute the sea batteries to the north of the city, and if approachable near. Discover if the Dey is popular or not, and the character of his probable successor. Find out if there is any particular person likely to be bold enough to take a popular lead in the event of any public clamour.

You may possibly be able, by putting on a jacket, to get a good view from your main-top with a glass, by loosing sails, and hiding yourself from view at a convenient time.

Get an account of the slaves, and if quiet or disturbed; and how situated.

As your great object is to conceal all this from the consul, who will take alarm easily for his personal safety, you must be careful to avoid giving any idea of intention in our Government to interfere; merely saying you should think it against our interest, who have very little to complain of; and if the continuance of the squadron is observed upon, you will say it is connected with the arrangement making for the Ionian Islands, and that you believe that Sir Thomas Maitland and Lord Exmouth are to be named in the new commission for arranging a new constitution, and a code of laws for the regulation of the Islands. At all events, you must carefully conceal your visit being induced but by common events, and with this management, and your own natural silence, I think you may escape suspicion of any design. You had better destroy this paper when you have read it; and you must be most scrupulously cautious not to betray by any possible conversation what our intentions are. Your going to Mahon is a mere cloak to avoid giving suspicion to any person about it; and the intention is known only to the secretary and yourself. You are called by every duty of an officer to keep the most inviolable secrecy.

Discover where the Dey's palace is situated, and take leading marks to direct shells to it; or any magazines of powder; or where the market lays.

Endeavour to discover how much powder and shot they may have; and of course you will minutely discover the floating force of all sorts, and how they are best got at, and if in any state of preparation.

Observe if the ship laying along the face of the Mole will be high enough to fire over it, if silenced, into the city; or if by placing one at a particular spot, the gate from the Mole into the city may be battered down.

Observe if a frigate or gun-boats may not be placed to advantage to the north-west of the Light-house and minute if any batteries could annoy them there, or prevent their firing into the Mole on that side.

Observe if there is any boom which would prevent fireboats from attempting the frigates or floating ships.

Observe the bottom, if good holding; and having satisfied yourself on these points, return and join me.

Be with the consul as much as you can, and go on board to write your observations, carefully locking them up. Be cautious never to have any sort of paper about your person which may lead to suspicion.

Exmouth'

Captain Warde wasted no time: by the end of February he was back at Livorno with a highly detailed report and an excellent chart. Subsequent events were to show the accuracy of his findings; even a brief extract indicates the wealth of fine detail which he recorded on his chart:

'12 A battery in good condition and well supplied. There are six

24-pounders mounted, and one dismounted, there not being room to work it in the embrasure intended for it. It forms three sides, with two guns in each: on the south side they point on the entrance of the Mole; on the east side they point into the Mole, and would annoy boats or men performing any service there. On the north side they point over the pier which joins the light-house to the main, into the bay in that direction. There is another gun, which points through a hole on the gates of the town, which is a curious piece or ordnance, having seven bores.

13 The gate leading from the Mole to the town, having four short guns pointing down along the pier; there are also two guns, about 18-pounders, pointing into the bay, to the north-west of the light-house.

14 A battery of four 24-pounders, and would bear on a ship coming into the bay, but she might get in so close to the pier between the light-house and the town, as to be out of its fire.

15 A battery having three sides, with two 24-pounders in each, pointing north-east, east, and south-east; the two latter sides would bear on a ship in the bay to the north-west of the light-house.

16 This is a large battery, with two tiers of guns pointing to the north-east; having nine 32-pounders below, and fourteen, either 24 or 18 above, with two guns on each angle. Those on the south-east side will bear on a ship in the bay to the north-west of the light-house. By rounding close to the rocks on the light-house side, a ship going into the bay would soon be out of the fire of the north-east face of this battery, but it is to be observed, that in taking this situation, a ship would receive the fire of between 90 and 100 pieces of cannon from the light-house, and other batteries. Under this battery, which is risen on arches from the ground, are 13 or 14 gun-boats; kept hauled up in the winter. There are also 12 or 14 lions and leopards chained up in this battery.'

Captain Warde noted all of this and much more, including an assessment of Algerine morale and soundings of the sea-bed, without betraying the fact that he was employed on an intelligence gathering mission. It was a noteworthy performance. Particularly astonishing is the fact that he identified the calibre and exact location of nearly six hundred Algerine cannon (one was twenty feet in length, the longest then in service anywhere in the world). If he could do this with only limited access to the town and its fortifications, we must assume that there were other pieces of ordnance which he failed to note. Hence the estimate by other observers (a total of one thousand cannon) is probably not far wide of the mark.

Exmouth studied the report, made his final preparations and then sailed from Livorno on March 4, 1816. After calling at Genoa and Port Mahon he arrived in the Bay of Algiers on April 1. His squadron consisted of five ships of the line, including the flagship HMS *Boyne,* and seven frigates and sloops. The British Consul, Mr McDonell, came off from the shore and consulted with the Admiral, giving him the latest intelligence of conditions in the city. The diplomatic aims of Exmouth's visit were fairly comprehensive: to obtain an agreement that the people of the Ionian Islands would have the same status in Barbary as British subjects, to sign a peace treaty with the Dey on behalf of Sardinia, and to sign a similar treaty on behalf of the Kingdom of the Two Sicilies. He duly went ashore and met the Dey and his officials. It was agreed that the Court of Naples would continue to pay a tribute of 24,000 dollars each year, the same sum as that being paid by Portugal. In return, the Dey agreed to release immediately 357 out of the 1,000 Sicilian slaves held in the city. Exmouth promised to pay 1,000 dollars per head for these released persons.

In the matter of Sardinia's interests, Exmouth secured the release of 40 slaves at a cost of 500 dollars each plus a cash bonus and various gifts. The Dey insisted upon cash in advance, so HMS *Calypso* was ordered off to Genoa to fetch the money and to bring back eight captured Algerine sailors whom Exmouth traded for 500 dollars per man.

On April 3 the two leaders signed a treaty in respect of the Ionian Islands and their people who would in the future be represented by the British Consul. No agreement was reached on the abolition of slavery or the release of any British subjects still in Algerine hands.

Having spent 373,000 dollars and having obtained the freedom of 397 non-British Christians, Lord Exmouth departed Algiers and sailed for Tunis. He seems to have gained confidence from his experience at Algiers in this strange business of haggling over the price to be paid for human lives. He succeeded in beating the market rate down to 250 dollars per head for Sardinian and Neapolitan slaves, while the Sicilian and Genovese nationals were freed without charge. He paid 66,750 dollars to ransom 267 of the former group and released 257 people of the latter. About 100 slaves from the Papal States were left in captivity. The Dey of Tunis did not promise to renounce all of his old habits, but he did state that future captives would be treated as prisoners of war rather than slaves. There was a cordial exchange of gifts and salutes and the British squadron sailed on to Tripoli.

The Dey of Tripoli followed the example set by his counterparts in Algiers and Tunis. Exmouth received a courteous welcome and he obtained the release of 414 Neapolitans and Sicilians, also 140 Sardinians and Genovese and a scattering of Germans and Romans. The total cost was only 50,000 dollars, a veritable bargain compared with the money paid to Algiers. Just as at Tunis, an agreement was made that the Dey of Tripoli would renounce slavery for all time, but allowance was made for the possibility that he might find himself holding prisoners of war from time to time.

Lord Exmouth now received fresh orders from London. The British government had seen his despatch regarding his negotiations with the Dey of Algiers and did not approve of the contents. Apart from his failure to negotiate a satisfactory treaty, he had paid a vastly inflated price for the unimportant group of Sicilian and Sardinian slaves, mainly fishermen and simple peasants, liberated in April. Worse, the British mission had been ludicrously ineffective when compared with that of the Americans, Decatur and Bainbridge, in the preceeding year.

Lord Exmouth himself must have felt the need to return to Algiers, with or without being prodded by London. Practice makes perfect and he was now becoming far more expert in dealing with these Turks. Tunis and Tripoli had agreed to stop taking Christian slaves, Algiers had not. Obviously the time had come to bring the Algerines into line.

The British squadron dropped anchor for a second time in Algiers Bay on May 14. Exmouth went ashore and had a long interview with the Dey. He opened the proceedings by presenting his government's protest concerning the terms of the treaty made the previous year with the United States. The Dey promptly took the wind out of his sails by blandly announcing that he had decided to annul that treaty and to declare war on the Americans.

Slightly nonplussed by this response, Exmouth launched into another protest, about the continuing enslavement by the Algerines of white Christians. For three hours Exmouth used all of his considerable debating talents to persuade the Dey that he should follow the example set by Tunis and Tripoli. Omar Bashaw was certainly swayed by Exmouth's arguments and he asked many questions concerning European custom in respect of the treatment of prisoners. Exmouth propounded the view that the future of Algiers should be based upon prosperity created by international trade rather than a continuation of the old Corsair tradition. He offered the veiled threat that rejection of this principle could lead only to armed conflict with a united Europe. Exmouth left this meeting with the clear impression that he had won his point.

The following morning he returned to the Dey's palace, accompanied by Consul McDonell, to find a totally changed atmosphere. His reception was distinctly cool. Overnight the Dey had met with his Divan and they had brought their leader back to earth with a bump. Exmouth's proposition was, to them, totally fantastic. He was suggesting that they should give up the easiest and most profitable way of life known to man. Worse, he was suggesting that the Algerines should indulge in work! It was unthinkable. The Dey made it clear to Exmouth that he could not sign the treaty which he desired. There followed four hours of argument which became increasingly heated. Tiring of the endless talk, Omar Bashaw then produced his trump card. He did not have the authority to decide a matter of such major importance; it would have to be referred to the Grand Signior in Constantinople. Only he could give a ruling, claimed the Dey. As we know, this was quite untrue. Algiers had been governing itself for many years past and the connection with the Sublime Porte was, to say the least, tenuous. Exmouth either did not know this, or he was tired and seized the excuse to end the interview. He agreed to the Dey's proposal of a six month's deferment, pending a decision from Constantinople, but he insisted that the Dey should then accept the Grand Signior's decision as being final. Omar Bashaw became very angry and made it plain that he would ignore the eventual reply from Constantinople, whatever it might be. Lord Exmouth now understood that he was being fobbed off with a meaningless excuse and he left the palace in a fury. His parting shot to the Dey was that he intended to break off diplomatic relations by withdrawing the British Consul, Mr McDonell. The reply, however, was that McDonell would not be allowed to leave the country without first paying his debts.

Exmouth started to walk arm-in-arm with McDonell down the narrow streets to the harbour, surrounded by the officers of his staff. A hostile crowd quickly gathered around them and they were stopped by a squad of soldiers who arrested McDonell. They even debated whether or not they should seize Exmouth himself, but eventually he and his officers were allowed to walk down to the quay where the cutter was waiting for them. It was a humiliating departure and a very tense situation had been created.

Although he could not have known it at the time, the action taken by Omar Bashaw during that hour was critical in its effect upon the history of Algiers. It was to result also in the eventual death of several thousand people. Infuriated by Exmouth's bullying, he called together his senior officials and gave orders that all persons of British nationality or protected by the British flag were to be rounded up immediately. Incoherent with anger, he gave orders which were open to a dozen different interpretations. Messengers were sent off in every direction, each conveying an order which reflected his own views as much as those of the Dey.

An immediate result of the Dey's furious instructions was the jostling of Exmouth and his party and the arrest of McDonell. Shortly afterwards another crowd of soldiers seized Captain Warde and Captain Riddell who were out riding in the nearby countryside. Dragged from their horses, they were robbed and knocked about before being escorted to the Dey's palace. Omar Bashaw's anger had by now started to subside and he was having second thoughts about the wisdom of an open dispute with Great Britain. Seeing the dishevelled condition of the two Royal Navy officers he apologised and thereafter treated them with courtesy. He sent out another group of messengers with orders to cancel the previous instructions. Unfortunately he overlooked the fact that a horseman had departed an hour earlier for Bone with orders for the arrest of all British subjects in that area. The Dey's neglect to cancel those orders was to have serious repercussions.

In the meanwhile Lord Exmouth had returned to HMS *Boyne* and immediately signalled to his squadron to clear for action and weigh anchor. His intention seems to have been an immediate bombardment of the town but, with the wind failing fast, his ships simply drifted away to the far side of the bay where they again dropped anchor. For the next two days Exmouth brooded on ways and means of securing the release of McDonell. Eventually he, too, regained his composure and was glad to accept a suggestion from the shore that negotiations should be re-opened. This time, however, he sent his brother, Sir Israel Pellew, to talk at length with the Dey. The Algerine was contrite and apologetic, expressing regret at the harsh things said during his encounter with Exmouth and attributing the clash to the deficiencies of the court interpreter. He renewed his insistence that an envoy should be sent to Constantinople but, regardless of the Grand Signior's response, Algiers would send an Ambassador to the Court of St James within the coming months to negotiate an agreement on the subject of Christian slavery. Sir Israel Pellew agreed to these proposals.

The vital fact was then disclosed that messengers had been sent to Oran and Bone with orders for the arrest of British nationals and persons enjoying British protection. Sir Israel expressed his indignation and the Dey assured him that counter-orders would be despatched immediately. It does not seem to have occurred to either man that the counter-orders would arrive in Bone two or three days after the original instructions, the distance from Algiers to Bone being 250 miles.

Sir Israel reported back aboard the *Boyne*. He arranged a final personal meeting between Exmouth and Omar Bashaw so that the two principals could patch up their quarrel. They met on May 19, exchanged courtesies and parted on good terms. The Dey presented Exmouth with an Arab stallion, an ostrich and a decorated sword, while Exmouth returned the compliment by giving the Dey an ornate sword of his own. Later that day his squadron weighed anchor and sailed for Gibraltar where landfall was made on May 30. Four days later he sailed for England in company with HM Ships *Bombay, Berwick, Ajax, Leviathan, Montagu, Spartan, Clorinde, Arachne, Reynard* and *Calypso*. The squadron reached Spithead on June 24 and Exmouth hauled down his flag two days later.

No doubt he was heartily glad to be home again and to have left behind the murky environment which passed for the corridors of power in Barbary. The fact must be faced, however, that he had created a situation in Algiers which was now more confused than before his visit. McDonell had been released from jail but, with his wife and two children, was being held under house arrest in his country home until such time as his alleged debts had been settled. The family were in an uncomfortable position which could have been even more difficult if the United States Consul, William Shaler, had not taken such a close interest in their welfare.

Adding to Britain's embarrassment was the unpalatable fact

There were four boys in the Pellew family. The eldest, Samuel, served all his life in the Customs service. The second, Edward, became Admiral Lord Exmouth. The third, Israel, had a distinguished naval career and became Admiral Sir Israel Pellew. The youngest, John, a seventeen years old ensign in the army, was killed while fighting the Americans at Saratoga in company with Edward. Sir Israel is seen in this portrait wearing the gold medal and Lloyd's Patriotic Fund sword awarded for his services at Trafalgar where he commanded HMS Conqueror (oil attributed to Ponsford, by kind permission of Viscount Exmouth)

that Exmouth had agreed to place at the Dey's disposal a Royal Navy ship, HMS *Tagus,* so that a deputation could be transported to Constantinople to conduct what amounted to sham consultations on the subject of slavery. He provided the Algerines with a second ship, a transport, in which to convey the Dey's gifts to the Grand Signior. These presents consisted of jewellery, brocades, fine weapons, panther skins, two horses, seven ostriches, forty parrots, two live lions and two live panthers. Not least of the gifts was a group of forty Austrian slaves! That one of Exmouth's ships should be used to transport a gift of white Christian slaves from one oriental potentate to another was hardly in keeping with the spirit of his original orders.

Why should a fighting admiral of Exmouth's calibre decide to swallow these insults and turn for home? The answer must lie in the terms of the secret orders received at Marseilles during the previous September and these are no longer available. However, all the evidence suggests that those orders were vague and imprecise, giving only limited opportunities to Exmouth to exercise his discretion. Certainly he returned to England in some trepidation, fearing that he might be criticised for having exceeded his authority and having gone too far in the arrangements which he had made with Omar Bashaw. It came as a great surprise to him, therefore, on going ashore at Spithead, to be confronted by a flood of criticism for not having gone nearly far enough! One interpretation of his actions appeared in the newspaper Independent Whig

'You must know in England, long before this time, that our

Admiral has been honoured with a mission to the Prince of Ruffians at Algier, and that he has patched up a something, which is called a Treaty with him, as if the ringleader of a banditti of Corsairs would adhere to any treaty longer than necessary and a superior force compelled his observance of it. It is quite a farce to talk of a treaty with this rascal . . . Then as to those countries, on which it was designed by our wise governors to be conferred as a favour, they are loud in reprobating it. They think the benefit small and temporary, and the expense burthensome and lasting; and they know that the execution of the treaty, after all, will be so capricious, that unless every demand be backed by a British fleet, it will be very soon a mere dead letter . . .'

The trouble stemmed in part from reports reaching England concerning events at Bone. It will be remembered that Omar Bashaw had sent hurried orders for British subjects in that area to be detained, this following his row with Exmouth on May 16. The messenger reached Bone of May 23, Ascension Day, and the local soldiery immediately turned on the local Christians. Ten years earlier the Algerines had granted exclusive trading rights with Bone to the British government, these rights to include the valuable coral-fishing franchise along the nearby coast. The British themselves did not exploit the coral but rented the concession to the Kingdom of the Two Sicilies. Consequently it happened that there were several hundred Sicilian coral fishermen gathered on the shore to celebrate the religious festival. The Algerines fell on them in an orgy of killing and more than one hundred were slaughtered on the beach, the survivors being bound and flung into prison. When news of these proceedings reached England the fat was well and truly in the fire. On the face of it, the Algerines had carried out this attack on poor white law-abiding Christians in breach of the peace treaty which Lord Exmouth had signed only a few days earlier on behalf of the Sicilian government. It was a slap in the face for Exmouth, for England, for a friendly ally, and for Christianity. British public opinion was instantly aflame. On the Continent the episode brought further embarrassment to Lord Castlereagh who was the subject of much sarcastic comment regarding Britain's apparent unwillingness, or inability, to put down piracy and slavery in Barbary. With hindsight, much of this criticism was quite unfair: the massacre had been an accident and was the result of poor communications rather than evil intent. The

Dey himself was obviously dismayed by the turn of events and he hurriedly called the various consuls to his palace to explain what had happened. His excuse was valid but it did not alter the fact that many people now dead would have otherwise been alive and, in the final analysis, responsibility lay with him.

The British government was secretly pleased and much relieved by these developments. Omar Bashaw had delivered himself into their hands. The outcry following the Bone murders gave the perfect excuse to put aside all pretence at seeking a peaceful diplomatic solution to the Algiers problem. The government could now proceed to take whatever action it felt necessary to crush the Corsairs. Exmouth had hardly unpacked his sea-chests before he was called to the Admiralty for consultations. No record of his conversations there has survived, but he was without doubt an angry man. He offered to return to Algiers to complete the task he had started. His offer was accepted. On July 1 he received his appointment to lead an expedition to Algiers and their Lordships asked what force he would require. This apparently simple enquiry was not easy to answer.

Part of the squadron which Exmouth had brought back from the Mediterranean was still anchored at Spithead, held in quarantine and waiting to be paid off. In theory it should have been a straightforward matter to reprovision these ships and to depart at once for Algiers. England, however, was now at peace. The press gangs had been disbanded (Impress Warrants were no longer in force) and the law did not permit the Royal Navy to recruit any man who did not wish to serve. With certain limited exceptions it had become an all-volunteer service and there was no system of reserves (the army was much better organised in this respect). Lord Exmouth hurried aboard the four ships. He addressed the men, inviting them to sign on for an expedition to Algiers and appealing to their Christian ideals. The response was alarming. From the *Boyne* most of the Royal Marines contingent volunteered their services but scarcely a dozen seamen responded. The *Bombay* produced twelve seamen and only one third of her Marines (the majority asking to be returned to shore quarters). The response aboard *Ajax* was even worse, not a single volunteer seaman, and the Marines agreed to serve only on condition that they would receive honourable discharges at the conclusion of the expedition (an extraordinary state of affairs because Marines were employed on a regular seven years engagement). Finally, it was the same desperate situation in *Leviathan:* two seaman volunteers and only half of her complement of Marines.

The sailors understood the law just as well as their officers, and knew that once they had been paid off they were free to go ashore. This was quite definitely what they wanted to do. They were given their money and, within hours, Exmouth's well trained ships emptied and became silent. The same exodus happened time and again at Portsmouth and other ports as ships and squadrons returned to England following months and years of arduous service in far waters. After Waterloo the strength of the Royal Navy was scaled down rapidly, mainly to save expenditure, and there was a desperate shortage of men still willing to serve in the remaining active fleet.

Exmouth shifted his flag to HMS *Queen Charlotte,* a first rate battleship of 104 guns, commanded by Captain James Brisbane and built to the same design as Nelson's *Victory.* Exmouth's first action aboard was to inspect the ship's company and he was

July 17, 1810, the First Lord of the Admiralty signals the launching of HMS Queen Charlotte by hurling a bottle of claret at her bow while a military band plays 'Rule Britannia'. In 1859 she was renamed HMS Excellent, gunnery training ship, and survived until 1892 (National Maritime Museum)

appalled by what he found. She was 200 men short of her correct complement and, of those listed, sixty were 'from imfirmity, age and wounds quite unfit for the service'. These men were put ashore, as well as a number of children. The official list of the rejected people states the reason for individual discharge: 'foreigner', 'very old', 'dumb', 'lame', 'cripple', 'bad eyes'.

Another blow was the discovery that many of the ship's company were mustered with rates for which they were not qualified. It was found necessary to disrate sixty men from able seaman to ordinary seaman or landsman. Evidently Captain Brisbane had been obliged to scrape together whatever hands he could find, including derelicts who were simply grateful for the Navy's meagre victuals and slop chest.

On July 2 Exmouth conferred with the recruiting officer in Portsmouth and announcements appeared in the town that any seaman volunteering for the expedition would receive a bonus of two month's additional pay. The flag officer at Portsmouth was

Commander Constantine R Moorsom RN, captain of the bomb HMS Fury, commissioned his little ship at Chatham on July 5, 1816, and sailed immediately with a scratch crew to join Exmouth at Spithead

asked to assist, but he could find only fifty-two petty officers remaining in the harbour guard-ships. Exmouth appealed to the Admiralty in Whitehall and they directed Rear Admiral Sir Charles Rowley at Sheerness to take the complete crew from HMS *Forth* and put them aboard the first vessel proceeding to Portsmouth. As the days sped by Exmouth and his officers continued the frantic search for the hundreds of experienced seamen and gunners needed to man the ships and to give the venture a reasonable expectation of success. The grog shops of Portsmouth were visited by recruiting teams which rounded up the men paid off a few days earlier and who had already spent their accumulated pay. The attraction of a gratuity of two month's pay was a big factor in permitting the new squadron to be almost fully manned by July 10.

The problem of numbers had been almost solved, but the quality of these scratch crews was unknown. Many of the men were strangers to each other and to their officers. A great deal of effort would be needed to create, in a very short time, the cohesive fighting force required for a major battle. It was not a very promising start. The officers worked hard to keep pace with their Admiral's demands: interviewing recruits, ordering supplies, filling water casks, the hundreds of things to be completed before a squadron could safely put to sea and face whatever an enemy or the elements might hurl at it.

Although the officers were over-worked during the first ten days of July, they at least were delighted at having obtained appointments to Exmouth's squadron, besieged as he was by applicants anxious to serve with him. It was now a year since the return of peace to Europe. The Royal Navy had cut back drastically the number of ships in commission, large numbers being placed in ordinary (laid up) or taken to pieces (sold to the breakers). Hundreds of experienced and able officers who had learned their profession during the previous twenty years, who had entered the service before puberty, who had lived ashore for only brief periods and therefore knew no life other than the navy, found themselves on half-pay and facing a bleak future. Many were young officers, unfortunate in the vital areas of promotion, fame or prize money. With no enemies left to fight, Great Britain could offer few opportunities to the majority of career officers whose skills were superfluous to peacetime requirements. Worse still, there was a growing dislike of professional sailors and soldiers by a civilian population which was required to pay the taxes needed to sustain them. Only one year after Waterloo the Duke of Wellington was obliged to send many of his regiments overseas in order to conceal their numbers.

When news of Exmouth's impending expedition reached the coffee shops frequented by unemployed naval officers the effect was immediate. Here was a chance, probably the last chance for many years to come, to win fame and glory. The rush was on and Exmouth sailed for Algiers with officers who were largely unknown to him but who were full of fighting spirit.

He had asked for a force of five battleships with a proportionate number of frigates and lesser craft for his expedition. He already had the *Queen Charlotte* and the Admiralty gave him four more battleships, HM Ships *Impregnable*, 98, *Superb*, 74, *Minden*, 74, and *Albion*, 74. They produced five frigates, HM Ships *Leander*, 50, *Severn*, 40, *Glasgow*, 40, *Hebrus*, 36 and *Granicus*, 36, plus various sloops, bomb ketches and store ships. There were nineteen ships in all, half from Portsmouth Command and half from Plymouth.

The composition of this force is arguably the most intriguing aspect of the whole story. On paper, in terms of theoretical fire-power, it was too weak for the task. Exmouth knew that the Algerines possessed almost one thousand heavy cannon, sited in strong masonry emplacements, their aim undisturbed by vagaries of wind or tide. His own artillery was protected only by the timber hulls of his ships and their aim could be upset by the vessels' pitch and roll. Given these two basic disadvantages it would have been logical for Exmouth to seek parity of numbers when calculating how many cannon could be brought to bear upon his enemy. Obviously his most powerful batteries were carried by his five ships of the line, *Queen Charlotte, Impregnable, Superb, Minden* and *Albion*. Their total armament was 430 cannon of which only half would be pointing out to sea. Hence there would be only 215 cannon firing at the target and even this modest number would be reduced by battle damage.

To supplement the fire-power of his battleships, Exmouth had the five frigates carrying 202 cannon, half of which again would be pointing in the wrong direction. However, it was a golden rule that frigates, whenever possible, should avoid slogging matches with opponents more heavily armed than themselves. Frigates were designed for speed, for handiness, and to act as the eyes of the fleet. Comparatively light timbered, they were not intended to be employed as battleships. As a man who had spent most of his

HMS Glasgow, built only two years earlier, the most modern frigate
in Lord Exmouth's squadron, was one of the five warships to come
under his command at Plymouth. Built in pitch-pine, she had a
shorter working life than vessels made of oak. She was sold
to the breakers in 1828 (National Maritime Museum)

professional life in frigates, Exmouth was fully aware of their
sailing and fighting characteristics. Furthermore, both he and the
Admiralty must have recalled the fate of Captain Riou and his
squadron of frigates at the Battle of Copenhagen in 1801. Riou had
been killed and his four frigates badly knocked about when they
placed themselves before the guns of the powerful Trekroner
battery, a fortification not unlike those defending the port of
Algiers. Admittedly three of the frigates allocated to Exmouth's
force were of the heavier type (particularly *Leander*), but their value
lay principally in their shallow draft rather than in their capacity as
battering vessels.

The possibility of a major foray against the Algerines was a topic
often discussed when officers of the Royal Navy met informally
over the dinner table. The technical problems stimulated good
conversation and tested a man's professional competence. Several
years earlier Horatio Nelson had been asked how he himself would
tackle the problem. It was his opinion that a force of ten ships of the
line would be needed and this view was widely respected by his
contemporaries. Exmouth's request for such a small force
therefore surprised the Admiralty.

Why did Exmouth sail with only five ships of the line, which
appears numerically inadequate, and with five frigates, a number
which could be regarded as excessive? Why did he not have at least

HM Ships Fury and Hecla, the two most interesting vessels in Exmouth's squadron. Known as 'bombs', they were built to withstand the tremendous concussion from their 13 inch mortars. The exceptionally strong hulls made them ideal for Arctic exploration. In 1819 the Hecla sailed under the command of Lieutenant (later Admiral) W E Parry RN in search of the North West Passage. In 1821 both Hecla and Fury made a second search, again led by Parry, and in 1824 he used them for a third attempt. HMS Fury was wrecked in a gale but the gallant little Hecla survived to make one final epic voyage under Parry, his attempt to reach the North Pole in 1827. Here they are seen (Fury left, Hecla right) after conversion for Arctic work (National Maritime Museum)

three or four more major vessels with hulls designed to absorb the prolonged battering which they could clearly expect at Algiers? There are several explanations. He was a man in a hurry and did not have the time to create a larger force. He had in fact great difficulty in manning the ships which actually sailed: finding yet more men for additional ships might have proved impossible or at least caused intolerable delays. These were limitations over which Exmouth had little control. However, it must be remembered that the waters surrounding the port of Algiers were very shallow and there was scant room for manoeuvre.

If too many ships attempted to anchor in the small stretch of water not exposed to the enemy's main batteries, they would possibly collide with each other and would certainly obstruct each other's field of fire. On the other hand, if only a few large ships approached the shore they would attract proportionately more of the defender's fire and would suffer greater battle damage. Hence there was a need for the frigates which could dash in to tow them out of danger or draw off fire from the shore. With hindsight we can see that Exmouth's force was not as ill-balanced or inadequate as it first might appear. He weighed all of the factors in his mind and came to a balanced judgment: it was a calculated risk.

Finally, it is important to note that there is no record of any discussion having taken place regarding a military force to accompany the expedition. We know that Exmouth did specifically request the services of two companies of Royal Sappers & Miners.

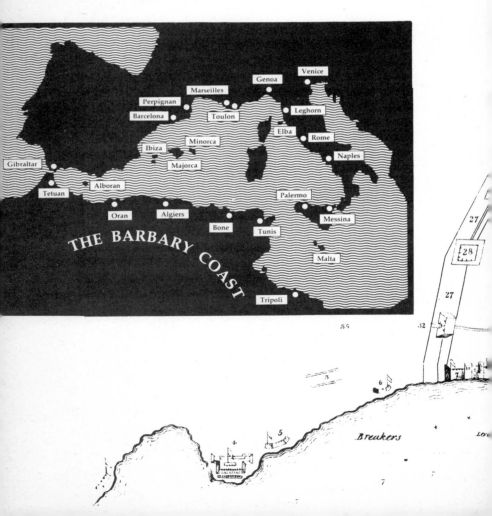

We know also that he had a force of Royal Marines under his orders, plus a handful of men from the Royal Horse Artillery. But he was not offered, nor did he request, any army units of sufficient strength to seize and exploit a bridgehead on an enemy coastline. He was not without experience in this type of operation, as we have seen earlier, and he must have known that only foot soldiers could capture and hold an enemy's territory. From the outset, therefore, this was to be a punitive expedition, not an attempt at conquest. The government, the Admiralty, Lord Exmouth himself, all must have known that the most they could hope to achieve was to give the Corsairs a thrashing and to batter their home port. There could have been no valid expectation that this venture would result in the permanent suppression of Christian slavery.

A cartographer's version of the plan drawn up by Captain Charles Warde RN during his secret mission aboard HMS Banterer in February, 1816. It shows Algiers' defending batteries, the inshore soundings and two lines of sight for a bombardment. The navigational hazards for a close approach are glaringly apparent

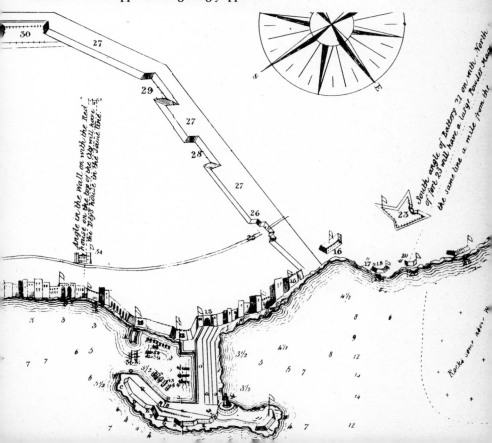

Algiers witnessed the first successful employment of the military rocket. On land it was issued to the Rocket Troop, Royal Horse Artillery, shown (above) in full review order on field exercises. The original Congreve rockets were launched from a simple frame easily installed in a small boat. Below, a 32-pounder is fired at a shore target while the crew shelter from the sparks of the propellant behind a sail soaked in sea water (National Maritime Museum)

CHAPTER FIVE

Southward bound for Barbary

DURING THE EARLY DAYS of July, 1816, Exmouth's ships at Portsmouth and Plymouth were completing the task of manning and provisioning. The cruise would not be a long one, large quantities of food and water were not required and hold space could be utilised mainly for the storage of munitions. Each ship took in powder and shot far in excess of the normal allowance. An unusual item of ordnance was a large quantity of Congreve rockets.

Certain experimental items were included in the inventories, among them a new type of carronade for *Queen Charlotte* and some prototype gun sights for the long 18-pounder cannon. The Admiralty had decided a short time before to conduct sea trials with these inventions and specialist personnel had been sent down to the coast from the Royal Laboratory, Woolwich, to supervise the trials. Suddenly these men found themselves embarked on an enterprise which would test their equipment under live battle conditions. The eleven technicians from Woolwich were the most surprised men in Exmouth's ships.

Already the admiral was forming in his mind a clear picture of the manner in which he would fight the battle. One of the orders he gave was that extra bitts must be fitted to the stern of each ship. These would enable them to anchor both fore and aft, with springs running from one anchor cable to another, thereby giving better fire control. Another measure in some ships was the replacement of hemp rope with chain cable. This reduced the probability of damage to moorings from close-range defensive fire by the shore batteries.

By July 10 the Portsmouth squadron was more or less ready to sail, although there were still serious worries regarding under-manning. The Commander-in-Chief at Plymouth, Vice Admiral JT Duckworth, did his best to find extra men from other ships lying in the Hamoaze. He also wrote to the Admiralty suggesting the transfer to Exmouth's squadron of men arrested by Custom and Excise officers for smuggling offences. The proposal was accepted and orders were sent to The Nore, Portsmouth and Plymouth, directing that all smugglers then in custody and fit for sea duty should be handed over to Lord Exmouth's officers immediately. This measure produced fifty men to be added to the growing muster lists of *Minden, Impregnable* and *Superb.* The *Minden* also received six convicted poachers from the local jail. The smugglers and poachers were the only non-volunteer ratings to sail for Algiers.

Apart from the men comprising the ships' companies, Exmouth was also allocated two contingents of specialists from the army. He embarked ninety-one men of the 7th Company, 1st Battalion, the Royal Corps of Sappers & Miners. They were commanded by five officers of the Corps of Royal Engineers, the senior being Major William Gosset, with Captain William Reid as second-in-command. There was in addition a party of nineteen men loaned from Major Elliot's Troop of Rocket Corps, Royal Horse Artillery, commanded by Lieutenant John T Fuller, RHA.

Exmouth returned from his final briefings with the Admiralty and the *Queen Charlotte* left Portsmouth harbour for Spithead. The Channel weather then turned nasty and stayed so for the next two weeks, the ships remaining at anchor until July 23 when the westerly gales finally abated and they were able to depart for Plymouth. During this period each ship was visited by the Commissioner's clerks who handed the men an advance of two months on their pay. The money was needed for their families ashore and for the purchase of personal kit from the bum-boats swarming around the anchored squadron. Even after these expenses had been met there were still relatively large sums of loose cash in the crowded mess-decks, a temptation to the thieves and gamblers aboard and a threat to discipline.

Owing to the delay imposed by the foul weather, any possibility of keeping the mission secret was lost. It now became public knowledge throughout the British Isles that Exmouth was bound for Algiers and this information soon passed over to the Continent. Initially, he had hoped to make a surprise arrival, before the

Algerines could have time to man the defences properly, but all hopes of that were now lost.

After their departure from Spithead the ships made slow progress down Channel, tacking frequently against the light south-westerly winds. One of these tacks brought them within sight of the crowds waiting on the Ness, a high redstone cliff overlooking the approaches to the Admiral's home town, Teignmouth. The vessels which sailed from Portsmouth were *Queen Charlotte, Minden, Albion, Severn* and *Granicus*. In company they had a number of smaller vessels, sloops and transports.

Before leaving Portsmouth the Admiral was fortunate in being allocated among the last-minute additions to his staff, an official Admiralty interpreter, Abraham Salamé, an exceptional man who kept a daily journal throughout the Algiers expedition. His descriptions of people and events provide one of the most lively accounts to be subsequently published. Salamé was a Levantine Christian who had travelled extensively throughout the Eastern Mediterranean and had worked in various capacities in Turkey, Arabia, Egypt and Italy. No stranger to war, he had served in various local campaigns with the Marmelukes and had a wide knowledge of the labyrinthine politics of the area. It is interesting to speculate what the outcome of Exmouth's earlier visits to Algiers might have been if Salamé had been with him then as an adviser.

It took Exmouth's fleet three days to reach Plymouth and they dropped anchor in Cawsand Bay on the afternoon of July 26. The cliffs of Mountbatten and the Hoe echoed to the sound of ceremonial gun-fire as Exmouth and Duckworth saluted each other's flags. Exmouth hurried ashore to confer with Duckworth and to find out what local arrangements had been made for the completion of his squadron. The vessels joining him were *Impregnable, Superb, Leander, Glasgow* and *Hebrus,* plus additional sloops and transports. Aboard *Leander* was Rear-Admiral Sir David Milne, the officer appointed to the expedition as Exmouth's second-in-command.

Although the squadron was now complete in ships, the manning problems still persisted. While final consignments of stores were being ferried out from the Royal Dockyard, the anxious business continued of trying to ensure that each ship had a full complement of men. Furthermore, it was vital that each ship should have a battle-worthy blending of experienced reliable men to offset the usual proportion of loafers and trouble-makers.

Parties of men were ferried from ship to ship, the numbers of seamen, gunners and petty officers being brought up to strength and each first lieutenant keeping an eagle eye open to ensure that his counterpart in the next ship was not simply offloading his own malcontents. Even at this early stage discipline was a problem, which was surprising, in an expedition that had been mounted on a volunteer basis. As early as July 20 the captain's log of HMS *Superb* noted the award of thirty lashes to a seaman 'for drunkenness and mutinous expressions'.

The squadron made final preparations, the last packets of letters and despatches were sent ashore and, shortly after mid-day on Sunday, July 28, Exmouth's ships weighed anchor. With the aid of an ebbing tide and a steady northerly wind, they formed up and set course for Cape Finisterre.

Later that afternoon the Admiral detached HMS *Minden*, Captain William Paterson commanding, with orders to press on with all despatch for Gibraltar. Exmouth intended that everything should be ready for him when the squadron arrived and he gave Paterson a comprehensive list of materials which he needed.

Abraham Salamé (left) described himself as 'a native of Alexandria in Egypt, interpreter in His Britannic Majesty's Service for the oriental languages'. Right: Admiral Sir David Milne poses for his post-battle protrait. In the distance, the port of Algiers engulfed in flames. He wears the sword presented to him by the Aldermen of the City of London

Exmouth was fully aware of the fact that his squadron was a make-shift force manned by crews of unknown and, in some respects, doubtful quality. He knew that this force would be faced with an immensely powerful adversary within the next four to five weeks. It was a dangerously short period in which to evaluate his officers and learn their strengths and weaknesses, and to impose his own personality and methods on the squadron. In this brief period he also had to train the crews to a standard which would keep them at their posts under every circumstance and regardless of fear, wounds and exhaustion. Even as he departed from Portsmouth he had given orders for an intensive programme of training which was maintained during the passage down Channel to Plymouth. The same orders were passed to the newly-joined ships at Cawsand Bay. Gunnery drills dominated life for officers and men alike as the squadron headed first west and then south into the Bay of Biscay.

The captain's log of each ship indicates the time and effort devoted to these drills. In the flagship, for example:

'**22 July** exercised great guns and small arms.
23 July exercised great guns.
24 July exercised Lower Deck guns and Marines.
25 July exercised Middle Deck guns.
26 July exercised General Quarters.
27 July exercised great guns.
30 July exercised a division of guns firing at a mark.
31 July exercised great guns.
2 August exercised General Quarters: fired six full broadsides: Royal Marines exercised with small arms, firing at a mark: exercised two divisions of great guns.'

Similarly, aboard the *Minden:*

'**2 August** exercised great guns and small arms.
3 August exercised great guns and small arms in the morning and again in the afternoon.
4 August exercised great guns and small arms.
6 August exercised great guns and small arms, morning and afternoon.
7 August exercised great guns and small arms. Fired six broadsides, three shotted and three with wads.'

These entries, and they are matched by similar entries in the logs of the other ships in the squadron, suggest that much of the drilling was carried out 'dry', the guns not being fired but the men going through the motions and developing speed and teamwork. The logs also make it clear that the Royal Marines were given intensive musketry training, the value of which became apparent later when they shot down scores of Algerine gunners and sniped the survivors.

Despite the fast passage, the hard challenging work and the warm pleasant weather, some of Exmouth's men succeeded nevertheless in falling foul of their superiors. On almost every day the cat o'nine tails was put to work in one ship or another. Noted in the *Minden*'s log:

'**5 August** seaman 24 lashes for skulking, seaman 12 for fighting, seaman 24 for fighting, seaman 12 for neglect of duty, Royal Marine 12 for quarrelling and abusive language'.

Noted in the *Glasgow*'s log:

'**1 August** seaman W Brown 36 lashes for theft, seaman George Delmar 36 for drunkenness, seaman Richard Symons 36 for neglect of duty, seaman Hans Lawson 36 for neglect of duty.
8 August seaman 24 lashes for theft, seaman 12 for neglect.
13 August 48 lashes and 36 lashes to two seamen for contempt shown to superior officers.
22 August seaman 36 lashes for drunkenness and fighting, seaman 24 lashes for insolence and contempt'.

Whether the crews were really as ill-disciplined as these punishments would seem to suggest is a debatable point. For almost twenty years the Royal Navy had been obliged to man its ships to a considerable extent with reluctant heroes, victims of the press gang and the sweepings of local jails. It may be that the officers and petty officers in Exmouth's squadron had not yet adjusted to the idea of volunteer crews.

While the lash was inflicting the first wounds of the expedition, the hazards of life at sea were causing the first death. On the first day of August a seaman, Martin Gordon, fell from the maintop of HMS *Glasgow* and was killed. His shipmates had little chance to mourn his death, even if they felt they needed to do so. There was too much work to be done before they reached Gibraltar.

While his ships' officers pressed forward with the training drills Exmouth was concentrating his mind upon a plan of battle. Anxious for the latest intelligence from Algiers he gave orders for all passing sails to be hailed and interrogated. Salamé noted in his diary,

'**Thursday the 8th.** In the morning came in sight of Cape St Vincent, we discovered a strange sail. His Lordship sent me on board with Lieutenant Johnson to get information. We found she was a Tripoline polacca called *Massadoda*, of 16 guns and 105 men commanded by Captain Omar, fifty days from Tripoli and five from Tangiers. The Captain knew nothing about the Algerines, and when I asked him for what purpose he came out of the Straight of Gibraltar, he was quite in confusion to answer me, and said, that he only came to look after some of the Hamburghers, Bremens and Lubeckers, for some old concerns they have with them.'

By August 6 the squadron was off the southern coast of Portugal and Exmouth had drafted his first set of orders and distributed them to his second-in-command, Rear Admiral Milne, and to the respective ships' captains.

6th August 1816. *Queen Charlotte* at sea.

General Memorandum
'It is the intention of the Commander in Chief to take his Station for the attack of Algiers, if the wind admits, as soon as the Ships arrive in that Bay, and the Dey's answer to his demand is returned, or the time for its reception elapsed.

If an attack is not immediately practicable the ships will, after they anchor, send their spare Topmasts, yards and Jib Booms to the Bombs and Transport as underneath, viz;

Queen Charlotte to *Beelzebub*		*Impregnable* to *Hecla*	
Superb	to *Infernal*	*Albion* to *Fury*	
Minden	to *Trafalgar* (transport)		

Ships will be prepared to Anchor by the Head or Stern as the prevailing wind may render necessary, and follow the example of the Flag Ship as nearly as possible if no positive inconvenience arises therefrom.

All boats will be hoisted out, the Launches prepared for the Howitzers and the Flat Boats for the carronades and Rockets, and the Jolly Boats must attend the latter with ammunition.

The Launches must be in the first instance prepared with hawsers in them ready to carry out Anchors, and not prepare for other service until the ships are all placed.

The Commander in Chief leaves to the judgement of the respective Captains the use of the iron cables. He means himself to bring up with rope cables, and when brought up — to lash the chains on the cables to ride by, paying out so much cable as will put them under water for safety from grape shot.

If the wind should oblige the Squadron to Anchor previous to any Attack, the Launches and the Flat Boats will be prepared for night service and care is to be taken to afford the crews as much rest as possible, and as the land winds generally prevail very early in the morning, the ships will carefully watch the Admiral's motions at night, and be ready to weigh at dawn of day.

Twelve pounds carronades having been supplied for the Barges and yawls, these boats are to be kept ready prepared to move in aid of, or protect the Launches on the least alarm, and will proceed to one of the two Brigs (which will, by signal pointed out have charge of the night) without delay unless called for by any heavy fire attacking the Boats already throwing Shell and Rocket.

Exmouth'

In addition to these organisational instructions Exmouth distributed a remarkably detailed order of battle, also copies of Captain Warde's secret chart.

6th August 1816. Queen Charlotte at sea

Form of attack
'The space for the attack on the south east end of the mole of Algiers being very limited, it will require the greatest attention to place the ships well in their respective stations; and it is very desirable to avoid opening any fire from them if it be possible before they are placed. But as it cannot be presumed that the enemy will remain inactive, it becomes necessary to prepare for that event by endeavouring to divert their fire from the ships of the line, by opening fire from the Frigates, which may under sail pass the Batteries in advance, or possibly in the intervals of the line as circumstances point out.

The Flag Ship will lead and bring up as near to the Mole Head as practicable. The *Superb* and *Impregnable* following will anchor as close as they can to her, the latter ship placing herself to the southward of the large arch near the centre of the works, and the *Superb* between us, and when placed, it will be of the greatest advantage, if they would be made fast to each other, and hove together to concentrate their fire.

The rear ship the *Albion* will see if by any failure she can supply the place of either ship thrown out. But if the *Impregnable* succeeds in getting her place it appears to me, the *Albion* may be well situated close on her bow presenting her broadside against the only flanking Battery marked 'A' of three guns, by which she may cover the *Impregnable,* and enfilade the North part of the works, by throwing part of her fire upon the upper tier of the Light House Battery.

The *Leander* will keep nearly abreast the *Superb* and seeing the Flag Ship placed, will anchor as near to her as possible, veering towards the town, until she opens the Mole, when she will either

93

fire on the Round Tower, or the Gun Boats and Batteries on the Town Walls. She must run a warp to the Flag Ship, and heave as close to her as possible to connect the fire of both, and to afford room for the *Severn* to get within her, or between her and the Flag Ship.

The *Glasgow* will anchor and present her Broadside to the Fish Market Battery No 9 & 10 and any others she may be able to fire upon.

The *Granicus* should occupy any space in the line open between the ships at anchor, or if either of the Frigates in the mouth of the Mole should meet with accident, she will endeavour to take her place.

Hebrus will attack Battery 7 & 8.

Minden will attack the large Battery No 4, taking care not to pass to the southward of the North East Angle, she will also be able to fire on No 5 & 6. This attack need not be closely pressed, being a cover only for the ships attacking the Mole from a flank fire. Captain Patterson will be extremely watchful of our operations, and be ready to slip and join, in the event of any accident to the ships attacking, and he will use the Schooner to the best advantage for communication.

Heron, Mutine, Cordelia and *Britomart* will consider it their first duty to attend and aid the ships they are named to assist in every possible way, and they are to remember that even their Brigs are to be sacrificed to save the ships they are ordered to attend; — should that service be uncalled for, by their being well placed, the Captains will take any position where their fire can be good.

Prometheus will tow down the Explosion Vessel, as instructed, and receive her Commander and Crew.

The Bombs will put themselves under the order of Captain Kempthorne, and as soon as anchored, prepare to open fire; they will be placed by the Master of the Fleet to the North of the large Arch, and take care during the attacks not to throw their shells over our own ships. The Light House Battery is a great object, and keeping that in line with the Tower Gates will give two objects for throwing the shells at.

Exmouth

NB Ships leading into anchorage are to have the preparation flag flying at the Mizen Top Gallant Mast Head, which is to be hauled down immediately they let go the anchor.'

These orders were amended and re-issued on August 13 at Gibraltar to take account of collaboration with the Dutch squadron found there.

It is indicative of his care in pre-planning that he called Salamé to his cabin and gave him an English draft of the letter of ultimatum which he intended to deliver to the Dey of Algiers, also the draft of a 'Declaration for the Abolition of Christian Slavery' which the Dey would be invited to sign. Exmouth was perfectly blunt with Salamé: he explained that he wanted these two documents translated into Arabic and Turkish before they reached Gibraltar. He intended then to show Salamé's handiwork to a languages expert who would advise the Admiral as to the accuracy of the translations. It says a great deal for Exmouth's character that he intended not only to verify the quality of his subordinate's work but that he have him advance warning of his intention to do so.

One of the pleasurable moments of the passage came on August 8 when the squadron was passing Cape Trafalgar at a time of day which happened to coincide with a routine gunnery practice. Salamé recorded in his journal that the ships' companies threw themselves into their work with enthusiasm and high spirits, making a game of imitating Nelson's cannonade of 1805.

One of the innovations tried out by Exmouth was a drill target invented a few years earlier by a young officer named Lieutenant George Crichdon. It consisted of a square framework of wooden lathes with pieces of cord running across from corner to corner and supporting in the centre a wooden bullseye. The whole device was three feet square and, during gunnery drills, it was swung outboard on the end of the foretopmast studding-sail boom. The first and second captains of each of *Queen Charlotte*'s cannon and carronades were given regular practice in aiming and firing at this gadget with an 18-pounder mounted on the flagship's quarter-deck. Aided by the innovation of improved gun-sights, they achieved a startling improvement in accuracy. By the time they reached Gibraltar the gunners were averaging ten hits for every fourteen shots, a respectable score in an age when broadside duels called for courage and speed rather than precision of aim. The bombardment of Algiers in the event did not require the gunners to be particularly accurate in their laying (apart from the opening minutes of the battle when visibility was still good). However, the drills did develop a keen competitive spirit between individual gun crews. Lord Exmouth had not always shown interest in matters of morale and man-management, but he noted that the development of Crichdon's target paid handsome dividends in terms of enthusiasm.

Arriving at Gibraltar, on August 9, and after the customary exchange of salutes, Exmouth went ashore to finalise the plans already set in train by Captain Paterson. One of the first tasks was to procure a number of flat-bottomed pulling boats and to convert them for use as gun and rocket boats. Similarly, the ships' long-boats were taken into Gibraltar dockyard and their keels, stems and transoms reinforced to withstand the shock of discharge by 12-pounder cannon and 24-pounder and 68-pounder carronades.

Exmouth had an unusually detailed knowledge of small boat construction and his ingenious ideas were put into practice swiftly by his ships' carpenters and the dockyard shipwrights. Their work was supervised in part by the artificers from the Royal Laboratory who had a special interest in the boats armed with mortars and the new Congreve carronades (which had yet to be tested in battle). They also had a professional interest in the Congreve rockets, supplied by Portsmouth and Gibraltar dockyards, which were still regarded as novel weapons. Subsequently, all these boats were rowed and towed a short distance out to sea and their weapons test fired. Nothing was left to chance.

Another requirement was an explosion vessel. The officer in charge of the dockyard produced a buoy-tender, HMS *Fly,* and she was loaded with one hundred and forty-three barrels of powder with the appropriate ignition fuses. This work was supervised by one of *Queen Charlotte*'s officers, Lieutenant Richard Howell Fleming, RN, aided by Major William Gosset, Royal Engineers.

Meetings were held between Exmouth's officers and other officers from the Rock to discuss the best method of destroying artillery protected by masonry. The engineers who were building the galleries in the Rock of Gibraltar had specialist knowledge which they passed on to Exmouth's people, and they carried out several experiments to test the effectiveness on stonework of differing calibres of ball propelled by varying charges of powder.

Dozens of small boats moved continuously between the ships and the shore. Quantities of shot and powder had been consumed during the last two weeks and the deficiency had to be made good. Fresh food and water were needed, plus an immense number of lesser items which might conceivably be useful. Contributing to all this movement was the flow of materials being taken out of the ships for storage ashore. Bombardment of coastal defences always invited retaliation with red-hot shot and the fire risk in wooden ships, full of cordage, canvas and pitch-impregnated timber, was immense. Exmouth gave orders that every ship should clear her 'tween-decks of all combustible items which were not absolutely necessary to sustain fighting capability. Cabin bulk-heads were knocked down and taken ashore, also great quantities of non-essential gear such as tables and stools. Personal sea-chests were stowed in the bottom of the hold and a platform built over them to accommodate the wounded. The sailmakers were employed in making canvas fire buckets; surgeons' mates counted their stocks of saws, ligatures and bandages; and the coopers inspected the water casks and powder barrels. Gun captains inspected the gun mountings for excessive wear after the hard usage of the past month's incessant drills. John Gaze, responsible for the safe navigation of the squadron along North Africa's treacherous coast, studied once again the charts and mariner's notes. Divisional officers conferred with their petty officers. Any men who were not fit for duty were weeded out and put ashore. The disorder and confusion of Plymouth and Portsmouth had been replaced with a taut expectancy of impending battle. What had been nothing more than a random collection of ships was fast becoming a formidable fighting force.

There was a brief pause when, on August 12, a 21-gun salute was fired by all ships and by the garrison battery to mark the Prince Regent's birthday. However, within two days of the squadron's arrival at Gibraltar the bulk of the work had been completed. Exmouth now gave instructions which, in the light of events during the actual battle, may seem strange. To quote from Abraham Salamé's journal,

'**13th August** — His Lordship gave orders to put in exercise all the boats of the fleet, with the marines, and the gunboats. It was a very pretty sight to see fifty or sixty boats in a line, in good order, with their different flags, regulating their fire by the word of command; and afterwards they all rowed towards the coast in order for landing, which formed a very interesting prospect'.

It is clear, therefore, that Exmouth did make provision against the possibility that he might be able to quench the Algerine batteries sufficiently for an armed landing to be made. However, this can surely never have been a central theme to his plan of action. In round figures he had one thousand marines and one hundred and ten military personnel. By stripping men from his ships' companies, and allowing for early battle casualties, he could have scraped together perhaps three thousand bayonets and cutlasses to form a storming party.

Exact figures for the Algerine forces are impossible to determine, but they are thought to have numbered approximately eight thousand Janissaries and fifty thousand irregulars scattered around the countryside. Only a complete collapse of the Algerine will to resist would have permitted Lord Exmouth to send in his landing party with any chance of success. It is fair to assume, therefore, that the drills witnessed by Salamé at Gibraltar were simply a reflection of Exmouth's life-time habit of carefully planning ahead and then seizing his opportunities as and when they arose.

Although in many respects a desirable quality, this characteristic allowance for every possible contingency may have done more harm than good in the context of the squadron's chain of command. Exmouth knew that he was embarking on an enterprise of the greatest danger. From the outset he understood the hazards to be faced, not only in general diplomatic and military terms, but also by each individual. The evidence suggests that he felt a strong presentiment of his own death. At Portsmouth he had written a letter to his son Pownall, instructing the young man to take charge of the family's affairs in the event that his father did not return from Algiers. Pownall was not permitted to join the expedition and his uncle, Sir Israel Pellew, was similarly excluded (despite his recent and intimate involvement in Algerine affairs). Apart from John Gaze and a handful of other trusted subordinates, Lord Exmouth deliberately left behind his close friends and relatives. Of the hundreds of officers who had clamoured for employment under his command, the Admiral had given preference to those whose death or mutilation would cause professional regret rather than personal grief. The vital appointment of second-in-command therefore, went to an officer whom Exmouth barely knew, Rear Admiral Sir David Milne.

Only a few weeks earlier Milne had received orders to sail for Nova Scotia where he was to assume command of the Halifax station. The ship in which he had been due to sail was the *Leander*. Consequently, when *Leander* was suddenly ordered to cancel her departure and join Exmouth's force, Milne found himself stranded. Rather than cool his heels in Portsmouth for several weeks, waiting for another ship to be found for him, he requested permission to stay aboard and to accompany Exmouth to Algiers. The Admiralty put this suggestion to Exmouth and he, a supremely confident man who had never placed great dependence upon his seconds-in-command, readily agreed. Milne meant nothing to him, either as a man or as a colleague. And so, by sheer coincidence, Milne's seniority placed him in a position which would have been critically important if Exmouth had been struck down at an early stage in the battle.

Milne was as pleased by the prospect of fame and glory as any junior officer. Here at Gibraltar he shifted his flag to HMS *Impregnable,* the second most powerful ship in the squadron.

Commanding the *Impregnable* was Captain Edward Brace, an elderly officer with a long and distinguished career behind him. Brace had been in poor health for some time and was on the point of retirement when, in early July, Exmouth told the Admiralty that he was one of the officers whom he particularly wanted in his command. Presumably this request was related to Brace's recent services in the Mediterranean: he had taken part in operations at Genoa and Gaeta. Unfortunately he was now back again, a sick man, serving under the immediate orders of Milne, an officer who was treating the expedition as an interlude before sailing to Halifax and who had no recent experience in the Mediterranean. We can only guess at the personal relationship between the two, but the erratic handling of *Impregnable* at Algiers suggests that there was a flaw.

Exmouth was continually in conference with his senior officers and with people from the shore staff during the four days at Gibraltar. There was one particularly unexpected but welcome encounter. One of the first sights awaiting him when he arrived had been a squadron of Dutch ships under the command of Vice-Admiral Baron van Capellen, his force consisting of his flagship, the *Melampus,* a 40-gun frigate, with four other frigates and a corvette in company. The Dutchman had been patrolling the Western Mediterranean for several months. His country had always avoided a head-on collision with the Barbary States, preferring to pay regular tribute since the late 17th century. However, following the fall of Napoleon and the restoration of the

Dutch monarchy, King Willem I adopted a tougher attitude and imposed a peaceful settlement with Tripoli and Tunis. Only Algiers remained as a threat to the East Indiamen on the trade routes of the Eastern Atlantic. Willem made a Proclamation that Dutch merchant ships voyaging further south than the Bay of Biscay must sail in convoy. At the same time, he despatched a small but powerful squadron to Algiers under the command of Rear Admiral Tulleken who patrolled the area unsuccessfully for several weeks before being sacked and replaced by van Capellen. The new commander was appointed in 1815 but the winter gales prevented him from resuming operations until the Spring of 1816. He brought his squadron into the Bay of Algiers on May 17, the very day on which Exmouth was preparing to patch up his furious quarrel with Omar Bashaw. The two Admirals met and compared notes; they even discussed the possibility of a joint attack on the city but decided that neither had their respective governements' authority for such action.

The Dutch did not participate in Exmouth's negotiations with the Algerines and it was only after he had sailed for England that they realised that he had taken no steps to secure Dutch interests in the area. There was widespread anger and resentment in Holland, Exmouth being heavily criticised for his failure to release any Dutch slaves or protect the shipping of a Protestant ally. The Dutch had been previously upset when the Americans made their own

Holland's conflict with Barbary began long before van Capellen's time. In 1624 a squadron led by Rear Admiral Lambert Hendriksz sank two Algerine privateers off Gibraltar. He carried 125 Corsair survivors to Algiers and, anchoring offshore, threatened to execute them unless their leader released his Dutch slaves and prizes. The Dey hesitated, so Lambert, suspecting trickery, killed all his prisoners. Some were hanged, others were bound back-to-back and thrown into the sea. Lambert briefly bombarded the city and set sail before the Algerines could retaliate. He encountered two more privateers, sank them and returned with more hostages. This time the Dey capitulated immediately (National Maritime Museum)

treaty with Algiers and Exmouth's behaviour seemed to be rubbing salt into that wound. Prior to Exmouth's return in July they continued to cruise the approaches to Algiers, hoping to browbeat the Corsairs into submission, but finding no real success.

When Admiral van Capellen heard of the expedition being mounted in England he took his squadron to Gibraltar to await Exmouth's arrival. An ardent Anglophile, van Capellen had had an extraordinary career spanning thirty years at sea and epitomising the shifting sands of Europe's confused politics during the Napoleonic period. In 1781 he had fought the British when, as Lieutenant aboard *Den Briel,* he had been involved in a fierce action with HM Ships *Flora* and *Crescent.* His gallantry on that occasion was recognised by the award of two shoulder epaulettes. By 1799 he had risen to the rank of Captain and was commanding the Netherlands Navy Ship *Washington,* flagship of Admiral Story, whose squadron was anchored in the Texel estuary. By this time Holland was virtually a puppet of Napoleon's French Republic. The Prince of Orange was living in exile in England and the officers and men of the Dutch navy were torn between their loyalty to the Prince on the one hand and their sense of professional discipline on the other. When, in the summer of that year, a British expedition arrived off the Texel, van Capellen and his brother officers found themselves in an impossible position. They could either capitulate and join the British cause, or they could fight the

Vice-Admiral Baron Theodorus Frederik van Capellen, Royal Netherlands Navy, the man whose moral courage ensured that Exmouth would have adequate fire-power at Algiers (Naval Historical Dept, The Hague)

British and help to sustain a regime in which they had no faith. After some parley with Admiral Lord Duncan they agreed to surrender without firing a shot, and to change sides. Twenty-five Dutch warships were handed over lock, stock and barrel, and several were purchased into service with the Royal Navy. The *Washington* was renamed HMS *Princess of Orange* and van Capellen passed the next fifteen years in British service. He was tried *in absentia* by a Dutch Naval High Court, stripped of his rank and condemned to be shot if ever captured by Napoleon's forces. He survived, however, and returned to Holland after Waterloo. He was accepted back into the Royal Netherlands Navy, was granted a

Baronetcy and promoted to the rank of Admiral. His first sea-going appointment was to take over as Commander in Chief, Mediterranean. It was fortunate for the outcome of the impending battle that van Capellen was such a strong character and so pro-British in his attitudes.

As soon as Exmouth returned from his first visit to the shore he received the Dutch admiral aboard the *Queen Charlotte*. A small, mild-mannered man of sixty-five, van Capellen was received with the customary fifteen-gun salute due to his flag and the ship's band played encouraging selections as Exmouth led him down to *Queen Charlotte*'s great cabin. The Dutchman explained the purpose of his cruise and the nature of the difficulties which he had encountered at Algiers. He offered to place himself and his squadron under Exmouth's orders for a joint venture against the Algerines. This offer was accepted on the spot and the little Dutchman departed in haste, shrouded in the smoke of another fifteen-gun salute, to prepare his own squadron for imminent action. It is an interesting commentary upon the contemporary exercise of maritime power that these two admirals were able to reach such a decision without reference to their respective governments.

By Tuesday, August 13, the combined fleet was ready to sail. At the last moment the brig-sloop HMS *Satellite*, commanded by Captain James Murray, arrived from Algiers with news of the latest developments in the city. Murray stated that the Algerines were aware of Exmouth's approach and were preparing for battle.

A strong easterly gale, a 'levanter', now interfered with Exmouth's plans and departure was delayed for twenty-four hours. Fine weather was vital for the next few days: fifty-five small craft had been fitted out at Gibraltar and many of these mortar boats, gun boats and rocket boats were under tow by the larger vessels. Even a summer squall would have swamped them. The gale soon blew itself out, the wind backed first southerly and then westerly, and the fleet weighed anchor. Large crowds gathered on the Rock to watch the beautiful sight as the ships tacked out of Gibraltar Bay. The days of intense preparation were behind them and the crews were at a high pitch of expectation for the great adventure which lay ahead.

With the steady westerly wind to aid them, they made good time and by the next day were level with the island of Alboran, one third of the distance to Algiers. It was shortly after this point that the fleet encountered the corvette HMS *Prometheus*, Captain William Bateman Dashwood commanding.

Dashwood went aboard the flagship and gave Lord Exmouth a detailed account of his extraordinary adventures during the preceding weeks. His news was not encouraging.

When the British government first decided to move against Algiers, it became obvious that steps must be taken to protect John McDonell, the Consul there, and his family. Exmouth had sent a secret order to Gibraltar, instructing Captain Dashwood to visit Algiers and to warn McDonell of the impending attack. Dashwood's task was that of persuading the Consul to abandon his official post but without in any way arousing the suspicions of the Algerines.

The *Prometheus* reached Algiers on the afternoon of July 31. His Sicilian Majesty's Ship *Cristina*, a frigate, had arrived from Naples the day before and was anchored in the bay. She carried a large sum of money, part of the annual tribute payable by treaty to the Dey. Dashwood conferred with the Captain of the *Cristina* and was alarmed to discover that the Sicilians were well informed of Exmouth's preparations. Dashwood went ashore and, accompanied by McDonell, paid a formal call at the palace where he was received in audience by the Dey. The conversation was inconsequential, the Dey making no mention of Exmouth or the rumours in the town.

Dashwood tried to convince McDonell that he and his family should quietly slip aboard *Prometheus* while they still had the chance. The Consul, a man with a stern sense of duty, refused on the grounds that it was his responsibility, as representative of England's ally, the Two Sicilies, to deliver to the Dey's officers the treasure lying in the hold of the *Cristina*. Dashwood pointed out the apparent absurdity of handing over the money at a time when it might be used to strengthen further the Algerine defences against Exmouth's coming raid. McDonell insisted that he must observe the terms of the existing treaty, otherwise the Dey would have a ready-made excuse to move against British nationals and their allies in the area. Dashwood accepted the logic of this argument but pressed the Consul to get the business over and done with as quickly as possible.

For the next three days the Algerines played cat and mouse with McDonell, making excuses to avoid a meeting. Then, on August 3, a Spanish merchant vessel arrived from Genoa with the latest European newspapers and with packets of letters for the local Jewish merchants, all containing detailed warnings of the developments at Plymouth and Portsmouth. Another arrival from Marseilles was a French warship, the *Ciotat*. It was now common knowledge that Algiers was the target.

The Dey made no direct move against McDonell at this stage but a strong guard was placed around his house. Dashwood noted the military activity in the town and along the beaches and cliffs. The Dey had set the wheels in motion for a full mobilisation of his forces.

Dashwood succeeded in persuading the Consul that his wife and teenage step-daughter should go aboard *Prometheus,* but this was blocked by the Dey's orders. He refused to permit their evacuation until such time as McDonell had paid his alleged business debts of $30,000. The British lodged a formal protest.

By August 6 Dashwood was seriously worried: his small vessel was anchored within direct sight of nearly a thousand Algerine cannon. He developed a daring plan to rescue the McDonell family and to leave for Gibraltar that night. He sent two of his ship's gigs in to the quay, ostensibly to purchase wardroom supplies. Strolling past the guards surrounding the McDonell house, he delivered to the Consul's wife two midshipman uniforms. She and he step-daughter changed into these clothes and walked casually down to the quay where they boarded one of the gigs and were taken out to the *Prometheus*. The guards had suspected nothing, but there was still the problem of the baby.

Dashwood had discussed this matter with his ship's surgeon, David McManus, who suggested that he could drug the child with an opiate and smuggle it off from the shore in a basket. McManus went ashore with a party of seamen, collected the child and its Jewish nurse, and started back towards the quay. They hoped to give the impression that they were simply collecting supplies for their ship. Unfortunately the nurse had informed her Rabbi of the secret and he, terrified of possible repercussions for his own people, had told the Dey's officers. The party was arrested, along with the crews of the surgeon's gig and the second gig which the anxious Dashwood had sent back to the shore after rescuing the women.

On the following day Dashwood protested at the seizing of the baby. The Dey relented and it was handed over, but the men from the *Prometheus* were placed in chains in one of the *bagnios*. John

McDonell himself was arrested, fettered and held prisoner in his own house.

Captain Dashwood stayed on for a few more days, hoping to persuade the Algerines to release his men. By August 11 it was obvious that he would not succeed and he set sail for Gibraltar while he still had the chance to do so. Luckily his course converged with that of Exmouth's fleet.

The admiral digested the implications of this latest development. Even at this early stage of the game, Omar Bashaw had taken two of Exmouth's pawns: John McDonell and the twenty officers and men of the *Prometheus*. He was duty-bound to attempt their release by diplomacy, if at all possible, before launching his assault.

Adding to Exmouth's worries, the weather turned sour on him on August 24. For two days the wind blew steadily from the east and the motley fleet tacked slowly along the North African coastline, finally making landfall at Cape Cazzina on the afternoon of August 26. This high promontory forms the northern arm of the broad sweep of the Bay of Algiers. With the wind veering to the south and then fading away to a faint whisper, the fleet crept past the Cape. One more day would bring it within sight of the city.

Commanded by Captain the Honourable Anthony Maitland RN and carrying a crew of 340 men, the 50-gun frigate HMS Glasgow cruises along the treacherous rocky coast of North Africa

CHAPTER SIX

The face of the lion

THE ALGERINES first saw the approaching Anglo-Dutch fleet on the evening of August 26. Lookouts had been posted high in the hills along the coast and at the extremity of Cape Cazzina. Through the haze of a hot and sultry evening the Algerines saw the white sails on the horizon, gleaming in the rays of the setting sun. Like the men of Devon and Dorset at the approach of the Spanish Armada, they lit great beacon-fires which blazed through the night and carried the warning deep into the hinterland and along the coast to Algiers. Alarm guns were fired to emphasise the danger. Excited crowds roamed the streets of the city, chanting their support for the Dey and calling on Allah to grant them victory. Omar Bashaw was carried through the streets in a torch-light procession and people struggled to touch the hem of his caftan.

Dawn broke cloudless on the morning of August 27 and the crowds moved to vantage points along the city walls and the parapets of the white flat-roofed houses. Confident and enthusiastic, they raised huge silken banners which stirred in the light breeze coming gently in from the sea as the sun climbed quickly above the horizon. It would be another very hot day. The city was ready and waiting, the batteries manned and the foot-soldiers placed where they could best repel any attempt at a landing. Many of those who could not fight, the elderly, the women and children, had gone inland into the hills. Most of the slaves had been removed from the *bagnios* and were also being held inland. The Algerine soldiers jeered as they watched the last of the Jewish merchants hurrying away from their shops with small bundles of precious possessions.

The first of the day's five prayers was duly directed towards Mecca and tall pillars of smoke curled slowly into the soft blue sky as the soldiery encamped outside the city walls prepared to break their fast. The scene was colourful, almost medieval. The Algerine style of warfare had not varied greatly over the previous two hundred years.

To the Dutch and British sailors, Algiers appeared as a splash of white and cream against the sun-baked brown of the distant hills. Shaped like an almost perfect triangle, the city rested on a broad base where the water-front buildings and fortifications spread themselves around the port area. Reaching high up the steep hillside, the outline then gradually narrowed to an apex crowned by the powerful buildings of the Citadel. Each side of the triangle was clearly defined by massive walls and fortified towers. On the peaks of several nearby hill-tops were more forts and watch-towers. Even from several miles out at sea, the sailors could study the imposing batteries which glowered black-eyed down on to the port's approaches. On a glassy sea, almost becalmed, they watched and waited as the coastal current carried their ships ever deeper into the curve of the bay and ever closer to these people whom they had come to punish. Very soon now the moment would arrive when one side or the other would feel obliged to make a move. That moment was not long in coming.

At six in the morning Exmouth sent for his flag lieutenant, Samuel Burgess, and his interpreter, Abraham Salamé. They were to go in one of *Queen Charlotte's* boats to join HMS *Severn*. The frigate was to tow the boat closer to the shore so that Salamé could deliver Exmouth's ultimatum to the Dey under a flag of truce. They were to give the Algerine no more than one hour in which to accept the ultimatum. At the end of that time they were to return to the fleet. A simple code of signals was agreed to meet the unlikely possibility that the Dey might give an answer before the time limit expired.

Salamé changed hurriedly into his best clothes and, with Burgess, went aboard the *Severn*. Word of his mission soon spread and the *Severn's* officers crowded around him. He noted their comments in his journal, 'Salamé, if you return with an answer from the Dey, that he accepts our demands without fighting, we will kill you'. The Levantine was delighted by their bravery and determination but, being a civilian, he failed to understand the true motive behind their joking threats. A diplomatic victory might bring honour to Exmouth, but no promotion for his officers and men.

Severn set her studding sails and moved closer inshore. A mile out she cast off the long-boat and Burgess steered for the harbour entrance. The time was eleven o'clock. He could only hope that the large white flag fluttering on a spar above his head would be understood and respected by the Algerines. He and his crew of six sweating oarsmen were soon well within range of the defending guns. Six muskets had been hidden in the bottom of the boat as a precaution against treachery, but these were unlikely to have had any practical value.

As they neared the mole-head, Burgess and Salamé saw another boat coming out to meet them. It contained the port captain. The two craft approached within a few yards of each other and Salamé shouted to the Algerine to keep his distance. The port captain asked why the British deputation was afraid. Did they think there was plague in Algiers? Salamé replied firmly that he had no fear of the plague but that he had no wish to join the boat's crew from the *Prometheus*. The Algerine seemed confused by this reply and made no response. He then changed the conversation to more cordial lines by enquiring after the health of Lord Exmouth. Salamé entered into the spirit of the game by enquiring into the health of Omar Bashaw. After this exchange of pleasantries, Salamé explained the nature of his visit and delivered Exmouth's letter of ultimatum by passing it across to the port captain at the end of a long pole. He stated that an answer was required within the hour. The Algerine protested that it was impossible to obtain a reply to such a serious matter in such a short period of time. 'Very well, we will wait two hours but no more,' said Salamé. He and Burgess were then invited to come ashore where they could wait in the shade. Exmouth's delegates decided that sunburn was preferable to imprisonment and gratefully declined the offer. Salamé handed over a second letter, this one being addressed to McDonell, and he enquired into the health of both the Consul and the men from HMS *Prometheus*. There was a further exchange of courtesies, the port captain exhibiting the nervousness of a man who must now face his chief with unpleasant news, and the two boats parted company. The English boat lay a few yards off the mole and here it remained bobbing around in the broiling sun for the next two and a half hours, an object of interest and derision to the thousands of onlookers who hurled down insults and abuse.

Lord Exmouth did not waste the intervening time. He despatched *Glasgow* to close with the *Ciotat*, a French corvette anchored in the bay. Captain Maitland manoeuvred alongside the Frenchman and persuaded Captain Ranoir to go aboard *Queen Charlotte* where Exmouth interviewed him. Asked the reason for his presence at Algiers, Ranoir was sullen and evasive. He stated that he had no specific mission. Exmouth later discovered that Ranoir was lying: he was there at the direct order of the King of France, to warn the French Consul and to arrange the evacuation of all French nationals from the city.

The northerly breeze gained strength as the morning wore on and Exmouth was able to gather his scattered ships into a more orderly formation. At ten o'clock all ships exercised at quarters, loaded their guns, swung out their boats and prepared them for instant lowering and action. The fleet moved closer to the shore and hove-to at a distance of about two miles from the mole. The four bomb ketches moved in even closer and anchored in the position which they were to keep throughout the following bombardment.

All the British ships had cleared for action but, given the measures already taken at Gibraltar, this was a formality. There were no bulkhead partitions to knock down; they had been left in store along with any superfluous trappings. Galley fires were left alight for an hour or so, Exmouth having given orders that every man in his fleet was to eat a proper meal at noon. As soon as the cooking was finished the galley fires went over the side.

There were several foreign ships in the bay when the fleet arrived, but their captains, seeing the activity aboard Exmouth's ships and the constant flow of signals between them, drew the obvious conclusion. They, and *Ciotat*, quickly weighed anchor and removed themselves from harm's way. The *Ciotat* remained anchored offshore until September 2. Exmouth never forgave her captain for having lied to him.

On shore there must have been much agitated discussion between the Dey and his Divan, but we have no record of their debate. There would have been those who counselled an immediate compliance with the British demands; others would have suggested delaying tactics, and others again would have taken a truculent stance. Despite the clear evidence to be gained by looking out of the palace windows and observing the manoeouvres of the fleet, there was reason to believe that Exmouth would back down at the last moment. This belief was fostered by past history, so many other fleets had made threatening gestures before leaving with their tails between their legs. The general mood amongst the Algerines must have been one of defiance. In view of what was shortly to happen, we must conclude that they simply did not believe that Exmouth would open fire on the city.

During all this time William Shaler, the American Consul, sat at the window of his house watching the movements of the boats and ships in the bay and jotting down notes in his diary. We owe much of our knowledge of the following events to this man's foresight in recording his immediate impressions. Most of the other consuls had departed for the safe inland areas, but the Consul of Denmark closed his own house and moved in with Shaler. They spent the morning chatting and drawing each other's attention to every fresh development as they leaned out of the window like two spectators at a public entertainment. At quarter past two, a fresh flurry of signals was seen to run from ship to ship and the allied fleet edged closer in towards the shore. Fifteen minutes later the long vigil of Burgess and Salamé came to an end: they decided that they had waited long enough, certainly longer than Lord Exmouth's instructions permitted, and that they should return to the *Queen Charlotte*.

Flying the pre-arranged signal 'no answer received' they turned their backs on the Algerine batteries and Burgess put his men to row the now much reduced distance back to the flagship. Salamé records that he did not enjoy this stage of the proceedings. He fully expected that someone ashore might show his dislike by putting a ball through his back. Salamé did not really believe that he had escaped unhurt until he felt the flagship's deck beneath his feet and he was presenting his report to Lord Exmouth.

Exmouth did not wait for Burgess and Salamé to return on board before putting into operation the next stage of his plan. As soon as the 'no answer' signal was reported, he made his own general signal to the fleet, 'are you ready?' Following the detailed plan which had been copied and distributed to each captain during the passage from Gibraltar, they signalled 'ready'. At half past two the flagship ran up a fresh signal 'annul the truce — hoist the jib'. Taking the van, *Queen Charlotte* paid off on the starboard tack and began to move ponderously but majestically towards the head of the mole. The ship was conned by the faithful John Gaze and his leadsman called the marks as they edged into ever shallower water. The breeze was falling away fast and it became questionable whether *Queen Charlotte* would reach her allotted position. Exmouth had drawn up a most elaborate plot of the precise position which each ship was to take and its captain told exactly where he was to go and how he was to get there. These instructions were based upon Exmouth's examination of Captain Warde's map of the defences and were intended to place the bombarding ships in such a way that they could wreak maximum damage upon the batteries but receive minimum defensive fire in return. For the first few moments it seemed that these instructions would be followed to the letter.

The admiral had changed into a fresh uniform and he stood by the quarterdeck rail, watching the approaching mass of the mole-head battery on which several hundred Algerine infantry and gunners were gathered. These men stood and gazed in wonder at the beautiful tall ship which was gently drifting towards them. The mole battery was very large and in height it exceeded the height above the water of *Queen Charlotte's* main deck. Hence the Algerines could look down at the British sailors standing around their guns, but they craned their necks to look up at the tops of the flagship's masts which towered high above them. Apart from the leadsman's chant, the silence aboard Exmouth's ship was total. The only voice on her quarterdeck was that of Exmouth as he occasionally muttered to himself. Salamé, always a keen recorder of other people's behaviour, noted a fierce intense expression on Exmouth's face, comparing it with that of a lion held in a cage and then set free. 'Never mind, we shall see now', murmured Exmouth. He turned to his officers, 'be ready'. There were just two feet of water between *Queen Charlotte's* keel and the sea-bed.

With her starboard side only fifty yards from the masonry of the mole-head battery, Exmouth gave the order to drop anchor, first the stern anchor and then, as soon as it held, the bow anchor. The cables were quickly adjusted to bring the main battery to bear upon the Algerine fortification. The sails were clewed up, not furled, removing the necessity to send any men aloft. The guns' crews stood to their weapons, motionless, waiting.

The flagship had been followed in by the other ships sailing in line astern: *Superb, Impregnable, Albion, Leander, Severn, Glasgow*. It had been Exmouth's intention that they should follow each other with the minimum safe distance between each and then anchor simultaneously in the same order when he made a general signal for them to do so. The rapidly failing breeze, combined with poor ship handling by Captain Brace in HMS *Impregnable*, broke the even spacing of the line. Captain Brace started to reduce sail too early during the approach and dropped behind his correct station. A large gap developed between his ship and the *Superb* ahead of him. Worse, when Exmouth anchored and signalled the rest of the line to do likewise, Brace followed the order literally and anchored his ship precisely where she was at that moment and without delaying long enough to recover the lost ground. Consequently the *Impregnable* took up a position where she would be completely exposed to fire from the powerful lighthouse battery and where she would be too far out to be able to concentrate her own fire in reply. Rear-Admiral Milne, standing at Brace's shoulder and ultimately responsible for the choice of anchorage, remained mute and failed to put matters right. A more forceful commander would have ordered Brace to shift berth and to comply with Exmouth's original orders.

The *Superb* followed in close behind *Queen Charlotte*, as ordered, but veered from her proper course, drifting to port and therefore away from the mole. She anchored too soon and consequently stopped in a position from which she could not give supporting and covering fire to *Queen Charlotte*. But at least she did occupy a berth from which she could enfilade one of the large mole batteries without herself being excessively exposed.

The *Leander*, meanwhile, had overtaken *Queen Charlotte*, passing down the flagship's port side, and went ahead one hundred yards before anchoring in a good position to rake the fish-market battery.

The *Minden* had followed in behind the main force and anchored close to the *Impregnable*, nearly five hundred yards out from the shore. Her captain, Paterson, soon realised the danger of remaining in such a vulnerable position and shifted his anchorage closer to shore, placing his ship astern of the *Superb*. The other vessels in Exmouth's squadron were still strung out in an untidy line-ahead formation, slowly approaching their appointed positions before anchoring, but slack sailed and unhandy in the dying northerly breeze. Before tracing their

City of ALGI

Remainder of Squadron under weigh

24 P^rs.
New Battery of 4 Guns
5. 18 Pound^rs.
4. 18 or 24 Pound^rs.
P
Ab
Fishers Gate
15 sma thro' a
Z
3. 24 Pound W.
Glascow
Gun Boats
Severn
Gun
Leander
Y
Boats
Gun Rockets
W⅓W
Dutch Frigate
7
7
Dutch Frigate
10
V
N
Queen Charlotte
Heron Brig
Dutch Frigate
SW
U
Hebrus
SSW
Granicus
W
5
Superb
X
Minden
Prometheus under weigh

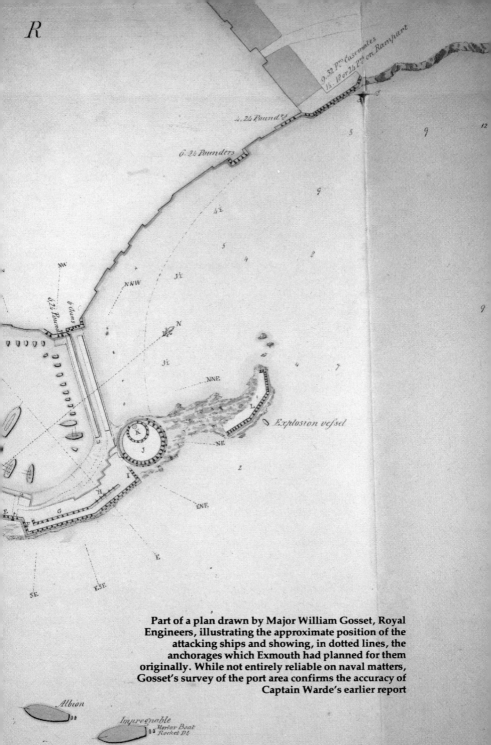

R

9. 32 Pr Casemates
1½. 18 or 24 P^r on Rampart

4. 24 Pound^{rs}

6. 24 Pounders

6 Guns

6 Guns

Explosion vessel

NW

NNW

N

NNE

NE

ENE

E

ESE

SE

Part of a plan drawn by Major William Gosset, Royal
Engineers, illustrating the approximate position of the
attacking ships and showing, in dotted lines, the
anchorages which Exmouth had planned for them
originally. While not entirely reliable on naval matters,
Gosset's survey of the port area confirms the accuracy of
Captain Warde's earlier report

Albion

Impregnable
Mortar Boat
Rocket D°

Mutine Brig under weigh

Infernal Bomb

individual movements we must return to the flash-point of the action, the head of the mole.

HMS *Queen Charlotte* lay huge and quiet beside the man-made cliff of the battery wall. Her crew shaded their eyes against the glare as they looked up at the heads of the Algerine soldiery lining the parapet of the top tier. It was an extraordinary moment in time: no noise, no movement, no certainty. Exactly what happened next is something we shall never know. There is no consensus of opinion.

Each eye-witness account varies in some particular from the next and is subject to vagaries of memory and individual powers of observation. Some accounts state that the fish market battery fired a single shot at the *Superb,* others state that *Queen Charlotte* was the target. Another account tells of a single shot from the mole-head battery hitting *Queen Charlotte* in the hull. One observer claims that the lighthouse battery fired three shots in rapid succession at the *Impregnable,* the balls flying wildly out into the bay. Whatever the truth, it is certain that at least one cannon was discharged by the Algerines and it is almost equally certain that this was caused by a nervous gunner who had opened fire without being ordered to do so. The commander of the Algerine artillery had failed to keep his gun captains in check. Accidental or otherwise, that first shot removed any fetters which may have been restraining Lord Exmouth up until that moment. He could now take the most vigorous action with a clear conscience.

Standing by the rail and staring across the few yards of water at his opponents, Exmouth had removed his hat and was holding it high above his head. Some of those present thought he was waving it in salute to the Algerines, others believed he was indulging in an act of humanity by warning the soldiers to move out of the line of fire. Whatever his purpose, the first crashing shot from the defences caused him to sweep the hat down past his waist and the officers commanding *Queen Charlotte's* main-deck battery took this as the signal to open fire. The flagship heeled gently to port as the 24-pounder carronades roared their first concerted broadside, followed in an instant by the two lower tiers of 18-pounder cannon. High in the cross-trees of the main-top and fore-top, 12-pounder carronades had been swayed up and mounted so that their muzzles could be depressed and aimed down at the open top tier of the mole-head battery. These pieces were each loaded with three hundred musket balls. The storm of

Under a skyline dominated by the Citadel and city walls, the fleet concentrates its fire on the mole batteries. From left to right, the HNMS Melampus, and HM Ships Minden, Albion, Queen Charlotte and Impregnable (National Maritime Museum)

metal discharged by them swept away dozens of the Algerine gunners who were running back to their cannon and leaping down through the embrasures of the lower tiers. To mount carronades in the cross-trees was not normal practice, but Exmouth knew that his main-deck guns could not hit the top tier of the Algerine battery and this was his novel solution to the problem. His inventive mind and foresight once again paid dividends.

The hours of gunnery practice in the British ships during the preceding days were soon justified. Broadside followed broadside in swift succession until gradually it settled into a long continuous roar as the better-served guns ran up, fired and re-loaded at a faster rate than the less efficient guns. It was now a matter for each individual gun captain to follow the drill as quickly as possible but without letting his men become over-excited. Fear or excitement could blind a man to the need for following the manual: neglect to swab out the barrel after each shot and retribution in the form of premature explosion was certain.

Within a few minutes of opening fire, *Queen Charlotte* had inflicted severe damage upon the mole-head battery. Some of the Algerine pieces were knocked from their carriages, the muzzles pointing uselessly at the sky or down at the water. Ball after ball was sent hurtling into the dark mouths of the embrasures and into the lower galleries, smashing men and equipment to a bloody tangle of limbs, splinters and broken stonework. The 24-pounder carronades were particularly devastating, being designed specifically for this kind of short range work.

The fire from the mole slackened and *Queen Charlotte* shifted her fire to another battery situated over the main gate in the city wall and facing the quay. Again her concentrated weight of metal had its effect, gun after gun being brought tumbling down in a shower of smashed masonry. An Algerine gunner leapt on to the parapet and waved his scimitar in defiance at the British as the cannon balls howled past his head. His surviving compatriots on the mole also showed their spirit by continuing to fire off those cannon which remained intact and sniping with muskets from behind cover.

While *Queen Charlotte* and *Leander* were setting their teeth into the defences, the other British and Dutch ships closed up, anchored, and joined in the bombardment. The first shots had been fired at ten minutes before three o'clock, but the last of the British ships to open fire, HMS *Impregnable*, did not join in the action until twenty-five minutes later. Each captain had started the approach with a clear idea of his own position, course and speed. These ideas were soon obscured by the dense bank of white smoke surrounding the first arrivals, *Queen Charlotte*, *Superb* and *Leander*. There now being only the lightest of breezes, the smoke discharged by their thundering guns, combined with that of the defences, lay like a thick fog around the mole-head area. Soon only the higher parts of each ship's rigging rose above this shroud. The 74-gun ships *Severn* and *Glasgow* crept slowly towards the white wall of gun-smoke, uncertain of what they would encounter once they had entered it. By great skill, combined with an element of luck, these two ships slipped past *Queen Charlotte* and *Leander* and succeeded in anchoring a short distance from the fish market and water front, the positions

118

which had been allotted to them in Exmouth's original orders. Here they were relatively safe from defensive fire and enjoyed a good selection of targets for their own guns. The third of the 74's, *Albion,* had initially followed *Minden's* example by anchoring close to *Impregnable.* Her captain, John Coode, quickly understood the great peril of this exposed position and he followed *Minden's* initiative by weighing anchor and shifting closer inshore to bring up astern of her. This left *Impregnable* isolated and exposed to the full fury of the Algerine batteries lining the mole and surrounding the light-house. Her only support was the tiny 18-gun brig-sloop, HMS *Mutine.*

The two smaller frigates, *Granicus* and *Hebrus,* inched their way into the cauldron of noise and violence at the mole-head and took station as best they could. *Granicus* anchored more or less in her correct place, ahead of *Superb* and astern of *Queen Charlotte.* *Hebrus,* on the other hand, veered far to port and finally anchored too far out from shore for her guns to be effective.

Captain George Bentham, commanding the brig-sloop *Heron,*

The scene on Queen Charlotte's main deck during the battle and showing the distinctive profile of the short-barrelled 24-pounder carronades. A marine and a sapper help to serve the gun on the left, while the hatless Lord Exmouth points out fresh targets from the quarterdeck (National Maritime Museum)

made his name by feeling his way far forward along the line of larger vessels and dropping anchor shortly astern of *Queen Charlotte* and in the position which it had been intended would be assumed by the vastly more powerful *Superb*. The little *Heron* played the role of ship-of-the-line throughout the long hours of the bombardment.

The remaining principal vessels of Exmouth's squadron, *Britomart*, *Cordelia* and *Prometheus*, did not anchor but moved around the area of the battle as best they could, firing at opportune targets and giving assistance to the many smaller boats which crowded the water like so many water-beetles. These were the oared gun-boats, mortar-boats, rocket-boats and barges numbering fifty-five in all. Many of these were in the charge of proud young midshipmen, most of whom were enjoying their first independent commands on active service. Together with the four bombs, *Beelzebub*, *Fury*, *Hecla* and *Infernal*, they lay off the port area and poured a deluge of projectiles into the town and over the mole where the Algerine shipping lay packed into the inner harbour. The rockets in particular were very effective against the latter target and many of the enemy ships were soon ablaze. The smoke from these fires joined that of the cannonade and the whole area became enveloped, literally, in the fog of war. At this stage it is certain that the two commanders,

Exmouth and Omar Bashaw, ceased to have any immediate control over the battle. Visibility was reduced to one ship's cable and less. This was now essentially a gunner's battle. The outcome would depend upon the ability of one side to fire longer than the other and to make its shots the more telling.

Crouched in the dark confined spaces of the main gun-decks, the British gunners served the long 18-pounder cannon in an atmosphere of suppressed excitement. There was an exhilaration, almost a frenzy, in the speed and physical violence which they applied to the endless rhythm of the drill: load, run out, fire, swab, re-load. The powder monkeys, mainly boys and landsmen, could barely keep pace with the speed at which the gunners were feeding the guns. They formed a human chain, passing up fresh charges from the powder lazarette deep in the bowels of each ship. In *Queen Charlotte* the gun-crews shouted for more wadding and, when it did not arrive in sufficient quantity, tore off their clothes and slashed them into pieces to pack the gun barrels. One man stripped off his jacket and rammed it home without emptying his pockets. As the gun fired he shouted, 'Damn my eyes, Jack, I forgot to take out my tobacco-box and knife!'

Almost naked, blackened with powder stains, streaming with sweat from their efforts and the extreme heat of the day, the gunners worked on, hour after hour. There was little need for fresh orders. They paused only to gulp a mixture of water and vinegar scooped with tin mugs from the butts lining the centre of each gun deck. Soon neither the gun captains nor the gunnery officers had any real idea of their fall of shot. Conversation was impossible. Orders were given by gesture and hand-signal. Men became deaf, many losing their hearing for several days after the battle, others never to regain it.

Deafness was the least maiming of the injuries suffered by Exmouth's crews. Battle wounds fell into three main categories: instant death when a man was struck by a cannon-ball in the head or trunk, amputation when he was struck by a ball in one or more limbs, and maiming caused by splinters of wood gouged out of

To the left (north) the British squadron lays clustered around the mole and port entrance. To the right (south) the Dutch squadron blasts the fish market batteries. The four vessels to seaward are the bombs (left to right) HM Ships Beelzebub, Hecla, Fury and Infernal the ship's structure by impact of heavy ball. Splinter wounds were amongst the cruellest of injuries, causing permanent blindness or making deep punctures which resulted in gas gangrene and a slow lingering death. Similar injuries were caused by grape shot or, as happened at Algiers, a mixture of musket balls, nails, broken glass, spikes and pieces of chain.

Abraham Salamé records that he was sent below by Lord Exmouth, the Admiral having noted his interpreter's terrified condition, and he made his way to the cockpit with the intention of assisting the flagship's surgeons. He stayed only a short while, being revolted by the stench and by the sights which he saw there. He notes one particular episode which moved him greatly,

'At this time I saw Lieutenant John Frederick Johnstone come down to the cockpit, wounded in his cheek. After he had been dressed, and remained for a short time, laughing at me, he asked me to help him to put on his coat, wishing to go on deck again. I then held him from behind by the shoulders to make him stop, and said: "Where are you going? You are wounded." In reply he said, "I am very well now, I must go." And so he went directly. After two hours' time I saw him, poor fellow, brought down to the cockpit again, by four seamen, with his left arm taken off quite from his shoulder, and it only hung by a little bit of flesh. When I met him in that horrible state he could not bear to be carried, but wished to be laid down where he was, and began to call "The doctor, the doctor". We all took care of him and the doctor immediately came and took off his arm quite from the joint of his shoulder. I saw that all the side of his breast was horribly torn. After he was dressed we laid him on a sofa with great care and we were all very sorry because we never expected that he would live.'

Lieutenant Johnstone in fact hovered between life and death for a week after the battle. Lord Exmouth had him taken up to his own cabin where, after the battle, the great man personally tended his young officer. Johnstone rallied and started to recover. He joked with his visitors and wrote to his friends in England. As the fleet neared England his ligatures burst and he died on October 3, being buried at sea south of Plymouth.

Lord Exmouth himself enjoyed no immunity from wounds and was extremely lucky not to meet his end on *Queen Charlotte's* decks. He was an obvious target for the Algerine snipers who were still crouched behind the shattered masonry of the mole-head battery. At least two musket balls passed through his clothing without touching him. Another shot smashed the telescope tucked under his arm. A spent shot hit his leg and drew blood, a splinter gave him a heavy blow on the jaw, and a musket ball broke the pair of spectacles in his jacket pocket.

Other officers had similar narrow escapes. Captain Brisbane was standing beside Exmouth when a spent musket ball struck the flagship's commanding officer and he fell to the deck. Exmouth turned to the Second Lieutenant, 'Poor Brisbane, it's all over with him. Take the command.' The captain sat up and said, slowly and deliberately, 'Not yet, my Lord'. A few moments later he climbed to his feet and resumed his duties.

The bombardment had been in progress for half an hour when the Algerines tried to spring a surprise blow against their attackers. A flotilla of approximately forty small vessels, galleys and gun boats, had been assembled on the hidden and sheltered landward side of the mole. These craft were packed with men and armed with small cannon. They suddenly rounded the end of the mole, heading towards *Queen Charlotte, Leander* and *Severn* with the obvious intention of boarding. The *Leander* was anchored opposite the entrance to the harbour and the miniature Algerine fleet emerged from the smoke into her line of fire. Captain Edward Chetham recognised both the danger and the opportunity. He shifted his gunners' attention to the approaching menace and a series of full broadsides caught the Algerines in a storm of grape and canister shot. The Royal Marines aboard *Leander* and *Queen Charlotte* added to the slaughter with volley after volley of musketry fire. Within minutes thirty-five boats had been smashed and the remainder turned and fled back into the harbour. They left several hundred of their compatriots in the water, either motionless or struggling for their lives. As John Gaze said after the battle, 'they might as well have endeavoured to board the moon'.

At around four o'clock, Lord Exmouth decided to deal with an Algerine frigate which was moored as a blockship across the mouth of the inner harbour. *Leander* was ordered to cease fire while the flagship's barge was despatched with orders to run alongside this vessel and destroy it. The barge was commanded by Lieutenant Peter Richards, RN, and carried a boarding party led by Major William Gosset, Royal Engineers, supported by Lieutenant Ambrose Wolrige, Royal Marines, and Midshipman Henry M'Clintock, RN. They succeeded in getting aboard the enemy frigate and fired her with laboratory torches and a carcass shell placed on her main deck. We are not told how the Algerine crew reacted to this invasion of their privacy: the adventure must have provided some stirring moments. Within ten minutes Lieutenant Richards and his party were back aboard *Queen Charlotte,* having lost only two men.

The blazing Algerine frigate broke loose from her moorings as flames burned through the ropes and she started to drift away from the harbour towards *Queen Charlotte.* Exmouth was obliged to cease firing and put his crew to shifting berth and preparing to fend off what was now in effect a fire-ship. In those tinder-dry conditions it would have been fatal for the flagship to have had any contact with the Algerine. Fortunately the blazing wreck drifted by at a safe distance and later disappeared into the smoke and the outer bay.

At half-past four a boat reached *Queen Charlotte* with a message from Rear-Admiral Milne on the *Impregnable.* He reported that he had already lost 150 killed and wounded, a third of the casualties being inflicted by a single explosion when an Algerine mortar shell came plunging down through her main deck, bursting with appalling violence within her hull. Milne was asking for support. Lord Exmouth immediately sent a boat to Captain Maitland of the *Glasgow,* ordering him to weigh anchor and place himself in the vicinity of *Impregnable.* Maitland did his best to follow this order, but the feeble breeze of midday had by now been beaten flat by the pulse of the cannonade and the oppressive heat of the sun. He succeeded in moving only a short distance before being obliged to anchor again. Even this slight adjustment of position was sufficient to place him in direct line of fire from the fish market batteries and within a few moments the *Glasgow* suffered more damage and casualties than she had in the previous two hours. Ten of her crew were killed, thirty-six wounded.

As the afternoon wore on, the damage inflicted upon the port area and its defences became increasingly severe. The batteries around the harbour had taken a heavy pounding and several had fallen silent except for brief periods when the Algerine gunners succeeded in getting some of their guns back into action. Other batteries, especially those placed higher up the hillside, were still largely intact and they continued to pour down a heavy plunging fire on the anchored fleet. The harbour installations and warehouses were thoroughly alight, particularly those containing the combustible materials used in ship building and repair. The attacking mortar-boats and rocket-boats became more adept at seeking fresh targets and judging their distances. At five o'clock they were still sending a constant shower of rockets and other projectiles into the Algerine fleet crammed in the inner harbour. In reply, the defending guns of the semi-circular lighthouse battery tried to drive off these small boats and, at the same time, continued to batter the lonely *Impregnable* and her small consort, *Mutine.*

It was in order to quench the fire from the lighthouse battery that Exmouth gave orders during the early evening for his ordnance vessel, laden with 143 barrels of gun-powder, to be blown up as close to the battery as she could be brought. She was the *Fly,* formerly a buoy tender at Gibraltar and manned by six volunteers from the local dockyard personnel there. She was now placed in the charge of Lieutenant Richard Fleming, RN. This officer, first lieutenant in *Queen Charlotte,* had been commanding gun-boat No 5 (nick-named *Invincible*) throughout most of the afternoon, moored under the flagship's stern and engaging any target which caught his attention. He set off with Captain William Reid, Royal Engineers, and they went aboard the explosion ship which lay waiting some distance from the shore and under tow by the *Cordelia.* They were quickly joined by Captain Herbert Powell, RN, a volunteer serving aboard *Impregnable* and sent by Rear-Admiral Milne to direct them to the place where they should run the vessel ashore. It was Milne's second major error of the day. Powell's presence on board the *Fly* created a conflict of judgement. His orders were to direct the vessel to a certain point, but Fleming's orders were that he should take command. Hence Fleming was nominally the captain, but he was receiving orders from a supernumary who was his senior in rank. The result of this poor arrangement was almost inevitable. Having been towed inshore by *Cordelia,* and despite the greatest daring and boldness by the three officers and their skeleton crew, the *Fly* was run aground in the wrong place. The helmsman received the order to turn 'port' from one officer, 'starboard' from the other. *Fly* came to rest near a minor battery which had already received a hard pounding and which was no longer offering any

Right: Congreve's rockets soar across the night sky, high over the mastheads of Exmouth's anchored squadron. Left to right, HM Ships Queen Charlotte, Granicus, Superb, Minden, Albion and Impregnable (National Maritime Museum). Below: a primitive but vigorous Dutch view which emphasises the part played by the flotilla of small gunboats. It also makes clear the great value, to the Algerines, of their lighthouse battery (Stichting Atlas van Stolk, Rotterdam)

great threat to the badly damaged *Impregnable*. Captain Reid lit the fuse and he and his companions hurriedly left the scene in a launch. Shortly after nine o'clock in the evening the little *Fly* exploded with a powerful roar. Some minor damage was caused to the Algerine battlements in the immediate vicinity but otherwise the explosion was ineffective in removing pressure from *Impregnable*. To a certain extent the venture was counter-productive because the Algerine gunners in the more distant batteries thought they had hit the powder magazine in one of Exmouth's warships. They gave a great cheer and continued to fire their guns with renewed enthusiasm.

Turning the clock back to the early afternoon, we must now trace the movements of the Dutch squadron. Admiral van Capellen had agreed to Exmouth's suggestion that his five

frigates would be best employed in suppressing the defences along the water-front to the south of the harbour. As with the vessels of the English squadron, the movements and station of each of the Dutch warships had been most carefully planned. They were to approach the harbour area in line-ahead from the south, passing one of the outlying forts, Fort Babazoun, and bombarding it as they did so. They would then approach the harbour defences as closely as circumstance and the shallowing water permitted before anchoring. They would engage the batteries of the fish market area and the southern city walls. In addition to making a contribution to the destruction of Algiers' defences, the Dutch fire-power would ensure that the leading English ships, particularly *Glasgow, Severn, Leander* and *Queen Charlotte*, would not be trapped by cross-fire from the west and

By late evening the stricken port area was producing an eruption of smoke which filled the sky for miles around. In the middle distance, the mighty Queen Charlotte and her consorts. In the foreground, HMS Impregnable and one of her rocket boats. On the right, the brig-sloop HMS Mutine, her shattered bowsprit trailing in the water (Bauer, Rijksmuseum, Amsterdam)

north. Despite some confusion at the last moment, when they were preparing to anchor, the Dutchmen succeeded in carrying out their instructions in full.

It had been van Capellen's intention that his flagship, *Melampus*, would remain in the key third place in his line of five frigates. Unfortunately, one of his captains anchored too soon and not sufficiently to the northward. This was Captain Pietrus Zievogel in the *Diana*, the leading ship in the Dutch line. His admiral responded by taking the point and leading his remaining ships past the anchored *Diana*. Shortly after three o'clock the *Melampus* collided gently with the leading British ship, *Glasgow*, her jib-boom projecting over the taffrail of Captain Maitland's frigate. In this position the *Melampus* dropped anchor and here she remained throughout the afternoon and evening. The *Dageraad* had followed *Melampus* in from the bay and she anchored shortly astern of the flagship. Behind *Dageraad* lay the already anchored *Diana*. The two remaining Dutch frigates, *Frederica* and *Amstel*, anchored further south and further out from the shore, but still in positions from which they could bring fire to bear upon the southern fortifications of the city. The sixth Dutch vessel, the corvette *Eendragt*, kept under way and patrolled off-shore in company with *Prometheus*, *Britomart* and *Cordelia*.

Although it was nothing more than coincidence that the Dutch squadron had happened to be in Gibraltar when Exmouth arrived there, and although he had never counted upon the participation of these additional frigates, there can be no doubt that they made a very valuable contribution to the bombardment. It is possible, even probable, that Exmouth would have emerged the victor even without the support of the Dutch, but it is certain that his losses in men and materials would have been much greater. The Dutch casualty lists attest to the active part they played in this action.

Viewed from the landward side the battle offered a magnificent spectacle. William Shaler and his friend, the Danish Consul, ignored the obvious dangers of their exposed position and remained at their window in the American consulate. Shaler continued to make notes in his journal,

'The cannonade endures with a fury which can only be comprehended from practical experience; shells and rockets fly over and by my house like hail. The fire is returned with constancy from several batteries situated at the north west corner of the town and from four heavy guns directly below my windows. These batteries are exposed only to an oblique fire and apparently have not suffered much. At five an attempt was made to renew the fire from the Marine batteries, but it does not continue ten minutes. At half-past seven, the shipping in the port is on fire. At half-past eight, the cannonade endures with unabated fury on the part of the English and is returned from the batteries in this quarter. The upper part of my house appears to be destroyed, several shells having fallen into it, whole rooms are knocked to atoms.'

Despite the immense weight of metal hurled at each other by the opposing sides, and despite the material damage and human casualties inflicted, the cannonade went on hour after hour throughout the late afternoon and evening. The sun disappeared over the western horizon and then darkness hid the hills of the sweeping coastline and the sea became black, losing its horizon and merging with an over-cast moonless night-sky. The eye of a distant observer, perhaps some miles out at sea, would have been drawn to a single brilliant point of light, a concentrated glare of flame and explosion. To the thousands of men who continued to feed that furnace, the passing hours made little difference to their duty. Whether Britons, Dutchmen or Algerines, they fought on with equal bravery and determination. Among the many personal accounts of the battle, not one contains a reference to the coming of night. The participants simply did not notice it. Within each ship the crew had two principal tasks: to carry powder, shot and wadding to the gun decks from the holds and lazarettes, and to carry the maimed and dying to a place of safety below the water-line. By ten o'clock in the evening the munition stores were almost empty and the surgeons' cockpits were full and overflowing. Exmouth's fleet no longer had the means to maintain the bombardment and the rate of fire started to slacken. As though by common agreement the Algerines reduced the intensity of their barrage also. Like two bare-knuckle prize fighters, the opponents had fought themselves to a standstill; they had exhausted their strength and were unable to continue this brutal slogging match. At eleven o'clock Lord Exmouth passed the signal for his fleet to cut their cables and withdraw to seaward. The instruction to abandon the valuable anchors was made of necessity: many ships no longer had capstans in working order, some lacked sufficient spare hands to man the gear.

The withdrawal was a slow and painful business. A light but steady breeze was blowing off from the shore but, with sails and rigging shot to pieces, each captain was obliged to save his ship as best he could. The hardest hit ships were towed off by the more fortunate; others laid kedges and hauled themselves away from the shore. Jury spars were rigged and the smaller vessels pulled themselves away with sweeps. It required two hours for the allied fleet to escape from the Algerine field of fire. The *Minden* was ordered to remain to the last so that she could provide covering fire and she succeeded to a limited extent, but the powerful Algerine battery, sited high on the walls of the Citadel, continued to pour a punishing fire on to the ships far below. Both *Queen Charlotte* and *Impregnable* were hard hit again during this stage of the battle. The Algerine batteries did not fall silent until one o'clock on the morning of August 28. By then the allied fleet had succeeded in reaching a point about five miles out in the Bay of Algiers where it anchored for the night.

As though to add to the fury of the bombardment, the

elements now made their own contribution. The breeze increased in strength and there was a violent thunderstorm. Continuous sheets of lightning raced across the sky and there was a heavy downpour of rain which served to cool the air and wash some of the blood from the decks. It was fortunate that the sea remained calm: the allied seamen were in no condition to make any major exertions that night. They had fought their battle and could point to the distant fires as proof of their success. Tomorrow would doubtless bring fresh trials and the need for further labours, but the immediate requirement was for sleep. This was granted to them eventually, but only after Exmouth's instructions that the wounded should be properly attended to and the worst of the damage made good had been carried out.

Exmouth was joined in his cabin by some of his officers and his old friend John Gaze. The chaplain led them in a short service of thanksgiving, and a few moments later Admiral van Capellen came aboard to offer his congratulations. Rear-Admiral Milne also joined the party in Exmouth's cabin, no doubt with mixed feelings about the reception which he might expect, but Exmouth greeted him in a friendly manner and no word was said regarding *Impregnable*'s performance.

Salamé records the scene, 'After we had anchored, his Lordship, having ordered his steward in the morning, to keep several dishes ready, gave a grand supper to the officers of the ship; and drank to every brave man in the fleet. We also drank to his Lordship's health, and then everybody went to sleep, almost like dead men.'

A detailed description of the battle was composed by Lieutenant John Whinyates, Royal Engineers, who was present throughout the day on the poop-deck of the *Impregnable*. Writing to a friend in England, four days after the bombardment, he set down his impressions of the hellish scenes in the 'tween decks. In the early hours of the morning of August 28, with the ship anchored out at sea and the night sky torn by the roar and flash of the storm, he chose to carry the lantern for Lieutenant Theophilus Beauchant, Royal Marine Artillery, who was making a round of the ship.

'The horror of the spectacle is difficult to describe. On the middle deck the first thing we saw was eight men lying between two guns, each in the convulsed attitude in which he had expired. One man had one arm extended, the other close to his breast, both fists clenched in a boxing attitude, whilst his right leg lay by his side, having been cut in two by a cannon-ball close to the hip. Near him was another poor fellow extended on his belly, his face downwards, with his back exposed: between his shoulders was buried an 18-pound shot. Legs, arms, blood, brains and mangled bodies were strewn about in all directions. You could scarcely keep your feet from the slipperiness of the decks, wet with blood. But a still more shocking scene was seeing the men and boys who had been burnt by an unfortunate explosion the main deck, crawling about the deck in the most excruciating agony, stark naked, a single feature of whose faces could not be discovered, perfectly blind, uttering the most heart-rending shrieks and cries, and calling out to everyone they met to put them out of their misery and put them over-board. Sixty unfortunate persons were killed and wounded by this terrible explosion. But this distressing and shocking scene fell short of what we saw in the cockpit, where three surgeons and three assistant surgeons were employed in attending the wounded, whose groans and shrieks and those of the dying pierced the soul to the quick. You tumbled at every step over the dead and wounded. One poor sapper, Andrew Mears, who was lying in a corner, and had been severely wounded at the commencement of the action by a grape shot through the thigh, on hearing my voice raised himself up, and forgetting his sufferings, eagerly enquired whether the company had landed and whether we had succeeded. Several were lying on the dressing-table, undergoing amputation or having their wounds dressed. I saw the whole process from the beginning, of one poor fellow's arm, a youth about 18, who used to wait in the Captain's cabin. He did not move a muscle of his face until the saw touched the marrow, when he gave a shriek which I shall never forget.'

The flash-burn injuries described by Whinyates were caused when the Algerine mortar shell smashed through the deck of *Impregnable* and exploded in the confined space of her main gun deck. The aftermath of that disaster, witnessed in the flickering light of young Whinyates' lantern as he stooped in the noise and stench of the lower decks, was part of the price of Lord Exmouth's success.

CHAPTER SEVEN

The calm after the Storm

WEDNESDAY, AUGUST 28, dawned cloudy and cool. The violent storm of the early hours had quenched the fires in the city and blown away the smoke of the cannonade. A light wind gave bare steerage way to the small craft which cruised offshore and ferried men and supplies betwen the ships of Exmouth's anchored fleet. Tired crews were stirred into movement and the labours of preparing their ships for whatever action the day might bring. The last reserves of ammunition were counted and prepared for a resumption of the bombardment, although the reserves were inadequate for more than a token attack. In terms of fire-power, the Anglo-Dutch fleet had shot its bolt. In contrast to the previous day's elation and excitement, there was a feeling of anxiety amongst some of the officers. It was difficult to see what further initiative could be taken if the Algerines continued to display the same spirit of defiance which they had shown throughout the bombardment. More than one officer expressed the view that the fleet had been fortunate to catch the late evening breeze off the land and to extricate itself without catastrophic loss.

On shore the Algerine soldiers also prepared themselves for another violent clash. The Dey was to be seen visiting his defences, encouraging his followers and urging them to fresh effort. As on the previous day, Omar Bashaw took a prominent part in the defence of the city and in making some attempt to repair the battered fortifications. The rank and file of his army remained cheerful and confident, but on the Wednesday morning there were signs that some of his officers and counsellors were losing their resolve.

William Shaler continued to write in his diary. 'Daylight exhibits the condition of the consular house. One room is completely destroyed by a shell, two others are in ruins, and a third and fourth very much damaged, my cabinet alone has escaped. The parapet of the terrace is partly destroyed, and the terrace is covered with shot and fragments of shell. The combined fleets are at anchor in the bay, apparently little damaged. Every part of the town appears to have suffered from shot and shells. The Marine batteries are in ruins and may be occupied without any effort. Lord Exmouth holds the fate of Algiers in his hands.'

This was the impression gained by Shaler from his window and his mistake is understandable. Viewed from a distance of five miles, the Dutch and British ships did not display their hurts. The American could not see into the empty lazarettes or into the over-crowded cockpits. Nor, fortunately for Exmouth, could the Algerines. The time had come for bluff to replace fire-power.

At eleven o'clock on the Wednesday morning a small boat was despatched, under a flag of truce, to carry a further ultimatum to the Dey. Just as on the previous morning, it was Samuel Burgess and Abraham Salamé who were selected by Lord Exmouth to act as his messengers. At about ten o'clock in the morning Salamé was called to the Admiral's cabin and told to translate the following letter,

'To His Highness the Dey of Algiers
Sir, For your atrocities at Bona, on defenceless Christians, and your unbecoming disregard to the demands I made yesterday, in the name of the Prince Regent of England, the fleet under my orders has given you a signal chastisement, by the total destruction of your navy, storehouses, and arsenal, with half your batteries. As England does not want war for the destruction of cities, I am unwilling to visit your personal cruelties upon the inoffensive inhabitants of the country; and I therefore offer you the same terms of peace, which I conveyed to you yesterday, in my Sovereign's name: without the acceptance of these terms you can have no peace with England. If you receive this offer as you ought, you will fire three guns; and I shall consider your not making this signal as a refusal, and I shall renew my operations at my own convenience.
I offer you the above terms provided neither the British Consul, nor the officers and men so wickedly seized by you, from the

William Shaler, Yankee sea captain turned diplomat who was US Consul
at Algiers from 1815 to 1823. After merchant service in China he
negotiated the annexation of the Hawaian Islands before being appointed
consul in Havana in 1810. Sent to Algiers by President Madison he was
outstandingly successful in securing American interests there. He died of
cholera in Havana in 1830 (painted by an unknown French artist in Algiers
circa 1818, photo by kind permission of the New York Historical Society)

boats of a British ship of war, have met with any cruel treatment, or any of the Christian slaves in your power; and I repeat my demand, that the Consul, and officers and men, may be sent off to me, comformably to ancient treaties.

Exmouth'

While Salamé settled himself to draft this letter in Turkish, Exmouth gave orders for the bomb vessels, *Beelzebub, Hecla, Fury* and *Infernal,* to move back to the positions which they had occupied during the bombardment and to make ready for a fresh attack.

As soon as they were ready Burgess and Salamé climbed down into one of *Queen Charlotte's* boats and were pulled toward the shore. Salamé continues his story, 'I was not so much afraid as yesterday, in consequence of the destruction of the batteries; yet, when we got rather near the mole, they fired three or four shots at us, from a castle at the south end of the fortifications; but fortunately these shots fell a few yards short of our boat. Upon this, we stopped, and began to think, very seriously.'

We must sympathise with his dilemma.

While waiting indecisively near the mole, Exmouth's envoys saw a small Algerine boat pulling out from the harbour. It contained a man named Omar Captán, the commander of one of the Dey's frigates which had been destroyed by fire during the bombardment. He and Salamé exchanged cordial greetings and the latter explained the purpose of his visit and gave notice that a reply was required within three hours. The Algerine remonstrated that this was too short a time limit. He explained that a full reply had been written on the previous afternoon and was ready and waiting for collection, but that he, Salamé, had failed to keep the rendezvous. Salamé swept this accusation aside and went on to complain at the morning's violation of his white flag of truce. Omar Captan apologised, 'Every thing happens by God's decree, and now, let us forget the past, and be greater friends than ever'.

The two men chatted for a few minutes before the Algerine turned back for the shore, leaving Salamé and Burgess to await a reply from the Dey. The British oarsmen pulled slowly into the mouth of the harbour where they could better examine the results of the battle. Salamé writes, 'During this time I was indeed quite surprised to see the horrible state of the batteries and the mole, since the preceding day. I could not now distinguish how it was erected, nor where the batteries had stood; as well as many fine houses which I had seen in the city the day previous. And I observed too, that they had not more than four or five guns mounted on their carriages, and that of all the rest, some were dismounted, and some buried in the rubbish. Besides this, all the bay was full of the hulks of their navy, smoking in every direction and the water out and inside of the mole was all black, covered with charcoal and half-burnt pieces of wood. But the most shocking and dreadful sight was the number of the dead bodies which were floating on the water. Among these bodies we saw a white one and afterwards, on finding it was one of our seamen, we took it with us on board.'

Less than two hours after the delivery of Exmouth's letter, three guns were fired by the Algerines. It was all over. Omar Bashaw had consulted with his Divan and they swiftly reached the decision that they could no longer resist the pressure of Exmouth's force and threats. The Swedish Consul was invited by the Dey to act as intermediary and he was rowed out to speak with Salamé and Burgess.

Burgess set his crew to row back to *Queen Charlotte* where Salamé hurried aboard to advise Exmouth of the latest developments. Moments later the Algerine boat came alongside and the Swedish Consul and the port captain, an Albanian, presented themselves to the Admiral. A boat arrived also from *Melampus* and Admiral van Capellen joined the others in Exmouth's cabin. After some tentative haggling it was agreed that all of Exmouth's demands would be met in full. Clearly there were difficulties. The British Consul, McDonell, was still in chains and held in a dungeon with a condemned criminal as companion. The slaves to be freed were being held some miles inland, scattered throughout the hill villages. The monies to be paid over to the British were also hidden for safety in various parts of the city and would need to be collected by the Dey's treasury officers. It would take time to complete these arrangements, claimed the Dey's envoys, and in fact little more was achieved on this day.

As shipboard life in the British fleet started to return to normal so did some of the officers settle themselves to the duty of writing home to England, reassuring their relatives and friends and stating their immediate impressions of the battle. Inevitably these

accounts contained some inaccuracies or did not agree one with another. The noise, the smoke, the excitement, such factors distorted the individual's point of view. But some of the most stimulating accounts of the battle were those written in the cramped gunrooms and wardrooms, still reeking of blood and gunsmoke, noisy with the hammering of the carpenters' repair crews on deck, letters dashed off in haste before the departure for England of Admiral Milne. He was sailing shortly in HMS *Leander,* taking Exmouth's official despatch to the Admiralty.

One such letter was written by Edward Trevor, midshipman, fifteen years of age and serving in HMS *Severn.* After telling his father that he was well and unhurt he set out the details of the voyage and the opening phase of the battle, then continued,

'We had scarcely one man left in our tops about 9 o'clock, and about half past 8 a shot came through the fore top sail into the foretop and took two men's legs off and sprung our main top mast, about three quarters past ten their battery began to slacken and at about 12 it was completely silenced for they had every gun dismounted. Almost the first shot that was fired struck the

138

The victory triggered a wave of artistic acclaim. This imaginative Dutch aquatint shows (left) Consul John McDonell reunited with his wife, daughter and step-daughter, (centre) Exmouth symbolically grinding into the dust a Turk scimitar while accepting the new treaty from Omar Bashaw, (in the archway) liberated slaves, and (right) Algerine treasury officials. Large numbers of this popular print were sold in Europe, but the scene is pure fantasy. No such post-battle meeting between the two principals ever took place. The Admiral acquired a copy of the picture, which must have amused him, for his own personal collection. It still hangs in the family home (Peduzzi, Amsterdam, by kind permission of Viscount Exmouth)

muzzle of my gun and hove the breech right off forward, but luckily did no other damage, presently after a shot came between the port and took a man's thigh off, and as I was standing close by one poor fellow a musket ball struck him in the stomach and he never spoke again. After the action which was about 12 we literally had not one whole rope in the ship. Our sides, masts, yards, sails and rigging, were as completely riddled as anything you ever saw, but notwithstanding we had next to the *Queen Charlotte* the very worst situation there I suppose we have fewer men killed than any ship in the fleet, only 5 killed and 33 wounded. At 12 after we had expended every grain of powder in the ship we were obliged to haul off and luck it was that the Admiral had just made the signal to that effect, so we all anchored again within about 4 miles of the Town. The next morning, what a sight there was, boat loads of dead going to be hove overboard and we could distinguish the dead piled up in heaps on shore.'

Extracts from another young midshipman's letter paint the picture as seen from the deck of *Queen Charlotte*,

'The Algerines suffered most of our ships to take their stations

139

before they opened fire, being confident of obtaining an easy victory over ships opposed by stone walls covered with guns. It is said that the first broadside from *Queen Charlotte* killed over 300 people and that *Leander's* destroyed as many more. From that time they gradually forsook their guns. The grandest spectacle I ever beheld was when their frigates were burning. This, together with shot, shells, rockets, etc, flying over our heads, has made so solemn an impression on my mind that it never can be effaced. None of us were hurt although the rigging over-head was coming down about our ears every instant, both these circumstances I account for by the supposition of their (the Algerines) firing uncommonly high, Queen Charlotte herself having not a man touched on her lower deck. Some say the battle of Algiers was at times hotter than Trafalgar itself. One of our Lieutenants, who was in that action, is of that opinion.'

The writer of this letter wrote to another friend, complaining that the Algerine gunners seemed to have 'learned the Navy list by heart, they took care to avoid every body who would have made a vacancy for promotion.'

One young gentleman who did come very close to vacating his appointment was Aaron Symes, a 23-year old midshipman serving as supernumary aboard *Hebrus*. The ship's flat boat had been adapted at Gibraltar for the launching of rockets and Symes was ordered to take command of this vessel as part of Exmouth's battle plan. As the bombardment opened he found a clear stretch of water, ahead of *Queen Charlotte* and astern of *Leander,* with a clear line of sight into the port area. With sixteen ratings and his friend Midshipman G H A Pocock, he spent the early part of the afternoon manoeuvring his small ship-of-war and gleefully despatching a shower of missiles into the packed Algerine shipping. His task was almost completed when he noticed *Queen Charlotte's* barge heading purposefully in towards the enemy frigate blocking the harbour mouth. This was the boarding party led by Lieutenant Peter Richards, RN, and Major William Gosset, RE. On impulse, Symes decided to join in the adventure and he set his men to pull for the shore. Unfortunately his track brought him into the sights of the snipers still infesting the shattered molehead. Despite shouted warnings from *Severn* and *Queen Charlotte* he held his course. The inevitable hail of musket fire killed Pocock and two sailors and severely wounded eleven others. Symes himself was shot in the hand and abdomen and a musket ball smashed his jaw, carrying away a part of his tongue. Somehow he rallied the three uninjured ratings and they pulled slowly back into the lee of the flagship.

Symes' action was foolhardy in the extreme and, given Lord Exmouth's reputation as a hard disciplinarian, he might have expected severe punishment. Instead he was rewarded with promotion and a grant from the Patriotic Fund. Exmouth took an indulgent view of the episode when describing it in his despatch, 'although forbidden, he was led by his ardent spirit to follow in support of the barge'. Symes was lucky, for Exmouth's mercurial Cornish temperament was not often so tolerant of disobedient subordinates. However, the Admiral had reached the age at which he could indulge kindly sentiments towards younger men who displayed dash and courage (and who were too junior to threaten his own reputation and position).

Aaron Symes subsequently regained his health and in the following year obtained a special Admiralty wounds pension of £91.50 per annum. Unlike most of his contemporaries, he remained in regular seagoing employment for the next thirty years. But now we must return to Algiers.

Thursday, August 29 brought a rapid increase in the pace of events. The British consul was released from his cell and brought on board *Queen Charlotte* where he gave to Exmouth a personal report of his recent harsh experiences. Admirals Van Capellan and Milne were introduced to the port captain, to McDonell and to the Swedish Consul. A negotiating party was sent ashore under the leadership of Captain James Brisbane of the *Queen Charlotte*, Exmouth himself declining to meet the Dey in person. The officers and men of the *Prometheus* were set free and restored to their ship. Rear-Admiral Sir Charles Penrose arrived from Malta aboard HMS *Ister*, commanded by Captain Forrest. He was too late to take part in the battle but was available to remove some of the burden from Exmouth's shoulders. Another arrival was HMS *Wasp*, commanded by Captain Woolridge. Her crew reported that they had clearly heard the thunder of the bombardment when sixty miles from the coast.

The outcome of the expedition was no longer in doubt and Exmouth was anxious to submit his report to the Admiralty. Late on August 30 he handed over his despatch to Admiral Milne with orders to sail in *Leander* for Gibraltar and Portsmouth. *Leander* departed Algiers with a favourable easterly wind behind her but, next day, the wind veered to the west. Exmouth guessed correctly that she would make a slow passage. He therefore ordered Captain Brisbane of *Queen Charlotte* to carry a second copy of the despatch to London overland. Brisbane handed over command of the flagship to Captain William Kempthorne of the *Beelzebub,* and then went aboard the fast sloop *Heron.*

HMS *Heron* set sail at 11.30 on the morning of September 1. Her commander, Captain George Bentham, had orders from Lord Exmouth to make his way as swiftly as possible either to Marseilles or Genoa and there to land his three passengers. They were Brisbane himself, his personal manservant and bodyguard Henry Chitty (formerly a steward in Exmouth's retinue), and a Dutch naval officer by the name of Lieutenant Pieter Arriëns. The latter was Adjutant on Admiral van Capellen's staff and he had been charged by his chief to carry the Dutch Admiral's own despatch to Holland.

The capricious winds of the Western Mediterranean soon played havoc with Bentham's plans. Just as a strong westerly was preventing Admiral Milne from reaching Gibraltar in HMS *Leander,* so was *Heron* meeting a steady north easter which pushed her far wide of the intended course. She gradually tacked away from the Barbary coast, but it required three full days for her to draw level with Port Mahon on the island of Minorca (where Bentham made a brief call). The idea of reaching the French or Italian coasts was abandoned. The anxious Brisbane requested that he and Arriëns should be landed somewhere, anywhere, and he did not greatly care which port was chosen as long as he could get ashore quickly and continue his journey.

At 9.30 on the morning of September 5 the *Heron* was approaching the Spanish port of Barcelona, her sails flapping in a dying breeze. Impatient to be on his way, Brisbane requested use of the ship's gig and had himself rowed into Barcelona harbour (accompanied by Arriëns and Chitty) while *Heron* crept slowly in past the outer mole. The two officers had been given a liberal supply of gold coins by their respective admirals and this money enabled them to hire a coach and driver for the next stage of the race. Motive power was provided by six sure-footed mules, the only draught animals which could be relied upon to withstand the hard climb over the mountains. Within an hour they were on

Pieter Arriëns, shown later in his career in Admiral's uniform. He raced to Holland with van Capellen's battle report

Sir Charles Penrose, at the end of his career in 1819. The face betrays his frustration and disappointment over the Algiers episode

the road, heading for the high passes of the Pyrenees. The roads had suffered badly under the passage of first Napoleon's and later Wellington's armies, and the corrupt Spanish administration had done little to repair the damage. Despite the hazards, the party reached Perpignan safely and here they bought a coach and four horses to take them northwards across France. After travelling day and night, frequently buying fresh horses and abandoning the exhausted ones, hiring fresh drivers as they went, the party arrived thankfully at Boulogne on Setember 13.

Lieutenant Arriëns parted company from his English friend. He sold off the heavy coach which had brought them from Perpignan and bought a 'tilbury', a light fast open carriage, in which to complete his journey. His adventures were not yet over. This part of Europe, in the aftermath of two decades of war, was infested with marauding gangs of scavengers — former soldiers and dispossessed peasants — who survived by theft and violence. Arriëns was twice attacked by such gangs on the road from Boulogne northwards through Flanders. Each time his carriage was overturned and only his sword saved him from being murdered. He succeeded in reaching the Dutch Admiralty at The Hague, and safely delivering van Capellen's despatch, on September 16. The delighted King Willem rewarded the young officer with the Militaire Willemsorde 4th Class

Captain Brisbane and Henry Chitty, meanwhile, had found a brig at Boulogne to take them across the Channel to England. Brisbane arrived on the steps of the Admiralty in London on the evening of September 15. A happy but very tired man, he had travelled the eight hundred miles from Barcelona, traversing the

Pyrenees and the English Channel in the process, in only ten days. It was an astonishing performance.

Subsequently he received a cash reward of £500 for having been the first man to arrive in London with the announcement of a great and famous victory. The payment was made by the Treasury, acting upon an instruction from the Prime Minister, Lord Liverpool, who received the recommendation from the First Lord of the Admiralty, Lord Melville. This unusual payment was based upon the precedent of Lieutenant John La Penotiere, commanding the schooner *Pickle,* who had been the first man to land in England with news of Nelson's victory at Trafalgar in 1805, and who likewise had been paid £500 and promoted for his services. The rarity of such cash payments emphasises the political importance attaching to Exmouth's triumph.

The Secretary to the Lords of the Admiralty scanned through Exmouth's report and called in the government printers, Mottley & Harrison, who worked through the night. Next day, a Sunday, a *London Gazette Extraordinary* was on sale in the streets with a full account of the battle.

In the meantime, Admiral Milne, who did not enjoy the best of luck during the expedition, had made slow time to Gibraltar. *Leander* anchored in Rosas Bay on September 11, only a few hours ahead of the bulk of Exmouth's squadron. Transferring his flag from the battle-damaged *Leander* to the faster *Glasgow,* Milne departed for Portsmouth on September 12 and finally reached London fifteen days later. He must have felt that his arrival was something of an anti-climax.

Back at Algiers, on the third morning after the battle, Admiral Penrose took over the task of visiting the Dey's palace and finalising the terms of the peace treaty. The terms imposed by Exmouth and in accordance with his orders from London were the following,

'Firstly, in the event of any future war between Algiers and a European power, none of the prisoners would be consigned to slavery but would be treated with all humanity as prisoners of war,

secondly, the practice of condemning Christians to slavery was formally and for ever renounced by Algiers,

thirdly, all slaves presently within the dominion of the Dey, regardless of their nationality, should be at once liberated and delivered over to Exmouth's officers,

fourthly, the Dey was to restore to the Italian States all the monies which he had received from them in tribute since the beginning of the year. This sum amounted to $382,500,

fifthly, a reparation of $30,000 to be made personally to the British Consul in respect of loss and damage to his own possessions,

sixthly, that the Dey should make a personal and absolute apology to Mr McDonell for the indignities and hardships which he had been obliged to endure,

seventhly, that the Dey should sign a new treaty of lasting peace with England, Holland and the Italian States and, upon the conclusion of these negotiations, there should be an exchange of salutes to signify the restoration of normal relationships between the countries concerned, the salute to consist of twenty-one guns being fired by each side.'

There were other matters at issue. Exmouth required an assurance, for example, that the *Falmouth* would be able to approach the mole, without interference, so that she might carry out the task of recovering the valuable anchors abandoned when the allied fleet cut its cables at the end of the bombardment.

The inclusion of *Falmouth* in his squadron was yet another example of Lord Exmouth's devotion to pre-battle planning. His memorandum dated July 7, 1816, requested 'that a sailing dockyard lighter should accompany the expedition for the purpose of carrying out anchors and assisting the ships in taking their positions'. The Navy Board had approved the request and instructed the port admiral at Portsmouth to allocate *Falmouth* for this duty. The important fact here is that Exmouth knew the layout of the Algiers port area, was aware of the limitations of space for his ships, and reasoned (correctly) that his captains might be obliged to cut their cables in order to withdraw or escape. Ships' anchors were not only expensive items to replace, they were vital for navigation along a dangerous coast, hence Exmouth's concern for their safe recovery. Dockyard lighters were specially ballasted and equipped with heavy lifting blocks and tackle: they could recover the heaviest anchors from the sea-bed. *Falmouth* was soon hard at work.

There was also the question of fresh water for the ships. Here the Dey could not assist. The city's aqueduct had been damaged by the cannonade. Pure water was a scarce commodity.

John Whinyates, the young engineer officer, was invited by Captain Brisbane to attend one of the earliest negotiating sessions as his personal guest. The captain had known Whinyates when the latter was a boy and the family connection gave him a privileged opportunity to record the scene.

'The Dey, Osman Pasha, a native of the island of Mytilene, and who had been Aga, or Chief of the Janissaries, was a fine athletic man, about 42 years of age, with a keen eye and an intelligent countenance. He was seated cross-legged, with naked feet, on his throne, plainly dressed, having a red turban on his head, another shawl around his waist, and he wore a pair of large loose Turkish trousers which came down to the knee. He smoked a long Turkish pipe with amber mouthpiece; the pipe was replenished thrice while we were there. His Chamberlain stood on one side of him and his Treasurer on the other. The pipe-bearer and a boy, or page, richly dressed, stood a little in the rear.

The Dey was cool and collected and made some very shrewd replies, evincing determination and courage, for the purpose of this conference was some fresh demands from Lord Exmouth. He replied that he would willingly fulfil all the terms of the treaty first agreed upon but, if the Lord Exmouth made new demands every day, it would leave him with nothing to exist upon and he would retire to the mountains and defend himself as well as he could.

In walking around the front and rear of the mole batteries, after the conference, I went into one of the casemates by a breached embrasure and was instantly turned out by some soldiers on guard. But I saw that the destruction of the guns and carriages had been great, and also the slaughter, for the back of the casemate walls was covered in blood and brains.'

The result of the discussions, in terms which would be most readily understood by Exmouth's political masters, was that the Algerines started to bring down to the waterfront the slaves who had been the original cause of the expedition. Salamé spoke with many of these people, some of whom had been in captivity for as long as thirty-five years and who originated from a dozen or more different countries. Most were in a wretched condition, particularly those who had no skills and who therefore had been employed in the most menial tasks. They were held in chains, these consisting of an iron belt attached to leg fetters. The slaves were kept in permanent groups of ten, each chained to his unwilling companions, and the group was in charge of a supervisor equipped with a whip. Hundreds of these people were herded down to the quayside, crying and cheering, shouting their thanks to Exmouth's sailors in a variety of languages, and waiting anxiously for the blacksmiths to strike off their shackles.

One of the British officers allowed ashore was Lieutenant Oliver Aitchison, Royal Marine Artillery, from the *Minden*. He interviewed a Frenchman who had just been set free after fifteen years in captivity. Aitchison asked the man if he hoped to return to France in the *Ciotat*, the French corvette anchored in the bay. 'No, never. I am ashamed of my country. But I would go anywhere in the world with the brave English who have so kindly liberated me.'

Elsewhere other slaves were being set free. The *Wasp* was despatched to Bone to collect slaves from that port while *Mutine* departed for Oran, to the west, on a similar errand. There is some discrepancy in the various published inventories of prisoners released from the three ports, but the following list is probably the most dependable,

Sicilians and Neapolitans	1,110
Sardinians and Genoese	62
Piemontese	6
Romans	174
Tuscans	6
Spaniards	226
Portuguese	1
Greeks	7
Dutch	28
English	18
French	2
Austrians	2
total	**1,642**

At first glance this appears to be a modest result for such a major effort. One is tempted to wonder whether the Algerines did indeed release all of their slaves in accordance with the treaty. The total of persons said to be held in the *bagnios* of Algiers itself was 1,083, yet it seems unlikely that such an important city could have sustained its economy upon such a small labouring base. However, the figures were sufficient to satisfy Exmouth and his officers and the various contingents were repatriated without delay. The Neapolitans and Sicilians went aboard the transports *Trafalgar, Maria* and *Friends* which sailed in convoy for Naples. Their escort was HMS *Severn* and she carried the Romans and Tuscans to the same port. The sloop *Wasp* embarked the Greeks and sailed for Malta and Constantinople. The Spaniards and Portuguese were put aboard the Spanish brig *Alexander.* The Dutch were put aboard the *Dageraad* which departed for Holland on August 31. Another Dutch frigate, the *Eendragt,* sailed for Marseilles to collect the new Dutch Consul, M Frossinet.

After the strain and exhilaration of the battle, Exmouth bent his mind to the immense volume of correspondence now demanding his attention. He settled himself at his desk in the flagship's great cabin, studying the reports of his subordinates and composing his own long report to the Admiralty. In addition, he wrote to the heads of the various governments whose citizens he had set free. It was his duty to describe his actions, and the results achieved, in language which would strike an appropriate balance between deference on the one hand and self-confidence on the other. As spokesman for His Britannic Majesty's Government, it was important to prove to the world that Great Britain had achieved a resounding victory. At the same time, any hint of arrogance on his part might create animosity, especially in France, and provoke political repercussions harmful to his own professional standing. A man of many parts, Exmouth once again displayed the skills of courtier, politician and author which he had developed over many years. His letter to the Pope, dated August 31, illustrates clearly his ability in this respect.

'Most Holy Father,
I have the honour of informing Your Holiness, for your satisfaction, of the success of the expedition against Algiers, which had been put under my command. The slavery of Christians is abolished for ever and, accordingly, I have the happiness of sending back to their families 153 slaves, Your

Holiness' subjects. I hope they will prove an agreeable present to Your Holiness and entitle me to be remembered in your efficacious prayers.

Exmouth'

The mind reels at the thought of a twentieth century officer of the Royal Navy being required to submit a report to Christ's Vicar on Earth on behalf of the British Government.

Salamé supervised the counting and weighing of the $382,500 which it had been arranged must be paid over to Lord Exmouth. The record states that the money was made up in sacks each containing $1,000. Fifty civilians were rounded up from the streets near the palace to act as porters, and the Dey's soldiers escorted them down to the harbour where the ships' boats were waiting to carry the sacks out to the *Queen Charlotte*.

It was then discovered that two Spanish gentlemen were still being held in chains in Oran. Omar Bashaw claimed that these men were under arrest for the non-payment of substantial trading debts. Admiral Penrose had a heated argument with the Dey who agreed eventually to release them. These and other negotiations continued for two more days, much of this time being taken up with protracted and tedious arguments over the final wording of the new treaty between Algiers and Great Britain, the establishment of a Dutch consulate with full status comparable to that of Great Britain's, the future representation of the diplomatic and commercial interests of Spain, Portugal, Sicily and other states, a settlement of accounts between these countries, and other matters which concerned the Foreign Office more than the Admiralty.

Penrose continued to lead the British team but he agreed to nothing without first consulting Exmouth. Consequently the talks dragged on for an excessively long time, while Penrose was ferried repeatedly between the palace and the flagship. Finally, to the great relief of both sides, all points of dispute had been resolved by the evening of Tuesday, September 3. At midnight the remaining ships of Exmouth's squadron set sail for Gibraltar (Admiral Penrose returned later to Malta with *Wasp* and *Ister*). Only Captain Dashwood in *Prometheus* was left behind to maintain a British presence and to give support to the much-abused Consul McDonell. For company he had Admiral van Capellen and part of the Dutch squadron (which remained at Algiers until September 9 before following the British to

149

Gibraltar for repairs and replenishment).

Exmouth reached Gibraltar on the afternoon of Thursday, September 12. Huge crowds waved and cheered and the garrison artillery fired three salvoes, of 63 guns each, from the North, Saluting and Europa batteries. Clouds of smoke drifted across the harbour as the ships came to anchor.

There was instant activity as a horde of lighters and small boats came out with fresh supplies of victuals and water. Dockyard officials consulted with ships' officers to decide what repairs were needed. The more seriously wounded men were ferried ashore for treatment at the Royal Naval Hospital. Eight of these men, mainly amputees and those suffering from burns, died in the following days and were buried by Chaplain M A Mackereth in South Ditch cemetery.

It required three days to prepare the ships for the passage to England and to re-embark the stores left ashore prior to the battle. On the third day a new arrival, HMS *Tagus*, brought the latest news from Algiers. Captain James Dundas had called at the battered port for a few hours on September 9, just as the Dutch were setting sail, and he had spoken with Dashwood of the *Prometheus*. He had also called at the palace and been presented to Omar Bashaw.

Dundas told Exmouth that the Dey was remarkably friendly and civil. The Englishman offered to place his ship at the Dey's disposal for the passage of officials to and from Constantinople, but the assistance was not needed. Dundas then walked around the shattered batteries and port area where the Algerines were busily salvaging some of their gunboats. Already some of the damaged cannon had been remounted on the mole. The city was calm, 'the agitation which the late events had created appeared to have entirely subsided'. Once again the Algerines were displaying their amazing ability to bounce back from defeat.

At four o'clock on the afternoon of September 15, again cheered by the local people and with a thunder of salutes, Exmouth's ships (including *Tagus*) sailed from Gibraltar and, by nightfall, had cleared the Straits.

All ships sailed in company northwards through the Bay of Biscay and into the Western Approaches. South of the Lizard the Plymouth-based ships parted company with much cheering and firing of salutes and turned north for home. On October 5 the battered *Impregnable* sailed into Plymouth Sound, followed by

Superb, *Hebrus* and *Beelzebub*, and the four moored to the quarantine buoys. An eye-witness reported,

'On returning to their station the ships saluted the Port Admiral who gave them a similar compliment. One general joy pervaded the three towns; the Plymouth bells pealed merrily and the Sound soon became covered with boats full of anxious inquirers for friends and relatives. On Wednesday the quarantine flag was lowered, and the *Impregnable* and *Superb* prepared to go up the Hamoaze. On hearing the signal gun, the inhabitants flocked from every direction to Mutton Cove, Mount Wise, the Hoe, and other eminences around. The wind was peculiarly auspicious and, as the vessels passed the Narrows into Hamoaze, with all the grandeur of British sail of the line, apparently as if conscious of the laurels they had so nobly won, the welkin rung with cheers from thousands of voices on both shores, and on board the shipping, until the *Impregnable* came to anchor off the Dockyard, and the *Superb* nearly opposite the Gunwharf. The *Beelzebub* followed soon afterwards, leaving *Hebrus* in the Sound, which came up the harbour on Thursday.'

Admiral Lord Exmouth sailed on up the Channel, reaching Portsmouth on the following day, October 6, just two months and eight days after the original departure.

To be set against his swift success there was inevitably a cost to be counted in both material and human lives. It is impossible to establish the exact scale of the Algerine casualties. The number of their dead was variously estimated at between 5,000 and 8,000. One report stated that 5,000 Janissary fighting men had died, also 5,000 Arab townspeople (including nine children sheltering in a room hit by a mortar shell). *Queen Charlotte's* first broadside alone is said to have killed more than 400 Algerine gunners and infantry on the mole.

The British ships suffered 128 killed and 690 wounded (of whom a significant proportion died during the following months or whose life expectancy must have been reduced by their mutilations and inability to earn a living). The Dutch ships lost 13 killed and 52 wounded. Hence the total casualties incurred by Exmouth's fleet was 141 killed and 742 wounded, with the hardest-hit ship being *Impregnable*.

Her starboard side was riddled by 233 heavy shot in her hull.

The report of hits on her masts and spars is equally impressive: foremast 6, bowsprit 3, foreyard 1, jib-boom 2, main-yard 2, maintop mast 3, maintop gallant mast 1, crotchet yard 1, gaff 1, main mast 15, total 268. None of these balls weighed less than 24 pounds. In addition, her sails were cut to ribbons, most of the rigging was shot away and large quantities of grapeshot were found embedded in her timbers. One shot, weighing 44 pounds, was extracted from the smashed woodwork by the crew, daubed with a slogan and slung in the boatswain's store, 'This was sent by the Dey of Algiers on board HMS *Impregnable,* as one of the advocates of slavery, but without effect, the 27th August, 1816'.

None of Exmouth's ships was dismasted, but their masts were in some cases severely weakened and their rigging much cut through. A new mainmast was stepped into *Impregnable* at Gibraltar Dockyard before she could continue her return passage to England. None of the allied ships or small boats was sunk.

The total cost of the expedition was estimated to have been more than one million pounds sterling. The expenditure in munitions alone was prodigious. According to Salamé's meticulous records, the British ships consumed 100 tons of powder during the battle and fired off 39,667 round-shot weighing 500 tons. In addition, the bomb-vessels threw 960 ten and thirteen inch shells into the city and several hundred rockets added their quota of destruction. The Dutch squadron contributed more than 10,000 round-shot to the barrage and, bearing in mind that all this metal and explosive was concentrated against one small city of 100,000 inhabitants, it is evident that Algiers suffered an immense amount of damage. Indeed, William Shaler wrote in his report to Washington,

'The city has suffered incredibly; there is hardly a house without some damage, and many are ruined. Great patience, time and expense seem necessary to replace their works in the state they were previous to the battle. Of their too celebrated navy, a brig, a schooner, and seven gun-boats only remain; of the latter, however, they are daily raising many which were sunk.'

Writing again on September 13, Shaler stated,

'The loss on the part of the Algerines is very great, certainly not less than 2,000. Much has been done to suppress Algiers as a

152

piratical power; all their ships are destroyed except the brig, formerly an American prize, the *James Madison* privateer. The ruin of the batteries is very extensive. They cannot yet know the greatness of their misfortune, but time will discover it for them. At present they are very anxious to appear undismayed, and they are actually fitting their two remaining vessels for sea with great activity.'

The loss in ships was in fact said to be five frigates of 44 guns, four large corvettes of 24 to 30 guns, thirty-two gun and mortar-boats and several small merchant vessels. The Algerines had saved two of their most valuable vessels by deliberately scuttling them in the inner harbour area, prior to the bombardment. Protected by their immersion against damage by fire and cannon balls, they survived the battle intact. Within days of Exmouth's departure they were raised, pumped dry and made ready for sea again. With these two exceptions, however, the Algerine fleet and its ancillary shore installations had been almost destroyed.

Against this background of ruin and desolation, it is interesting to find Shaler making a further report to Washington only six months later, on March 2, 1817, in which he stated that the Algerines had now completed the repairs to their defensive works. They had three ships in seaworthy condition and Omar Bashaw, who was clearly a man of energy and resource, was making a determined effort to restore the power and reputation of Algiers to that which it held prior to Exmouth's expedition.

On the day following Exmouth's departure, Omar Bashaw climbed to a high point on his palace walls and addressed the large crowd gathered in the courtyard. 'No, we are not vanquished! Or if we are, it is by arms which are unknown to us, those of corruption and treason. We fought like true Musselmen and our fame will be echoed on other shores. When the base perish they are no longer spoken of: the brave fall, their names are remembered and the glory of their country revives.'

The Dey worked hard during the following months to lead his people in the urgent task of re-constructing the city and restoring its commercial life. As we know from Shaler's account, he was outstandingly successful and this in itself is a puzzling aspect of the whole affair. How could the Algerines so swiftly repair the damage without the workforce of slaves rescued by Exmouth? If they had previously needed hundreds of slaves simply to keep the place in good repair, how could they possibly succeed in rebuilding the port, batteries and city in only six months without the brawn and skills of those slaves? Was the expedition really as successful as Exmouth and the British government claimed? It seems unlikely that Exmouth's officers could have thoroughly inspected all the *bagnios* and travelled extensively through the hinterland in search of hidden groups of slaves during the brief span between the bombardment and the departure of the fleet.

Logically, it must be accepted that Omar Bashaw may have retained a significant number of slaves in the hill villages, concealing the true facts from Penrose. Human nature being what it is, Omar Bashaw had every reason to lie and Penrose had every reason to ensure that his meetings with the Dey did not become too protracted. In the final analysis, the Royal Navy was more concerned with glory than social justice. Furthermore, it was the first duty of Exmouth's people to repair their ships and make ready for sea. Few officers were available for extended visits into the local countryside. They had freed 1,642 assorted slaves, an impressive number. Those responsible may have felt that it was sufficient to satisfy the politicians at home and to justify the effort involved.

Despite the rapid recovery of Algiers, the sands of time were fast running out for Omar Bashaw. Bubonic plague had again broken out along the Barbary coast. Life was hard for everyone, rich and poor alike, and the sentiment of the people started to turn against their leader.

On September 16, 1818, a delegation of Janissaries arrived outside the palace and demanded an immediate audience. The Dey enquired what it was that they were seeking. The reply was ominous, 'An individual from within'. Omar Bashaw sent messengers to the officers of the artillery and the navy, seeking their support, but they declined to become involved. The Dey understood that he too must now follow his countless predecessors who had suddenly lost favour. He swallowed a draught of poison. The Janissaries burst into his apartments and seized him and bound him with ropes. Omar Bashaw was already a dying man when his former supporters dragged him to the place of public execution and strangled him to death. The officers then returned to their homes to consider the matter of electing a new Dey. The whole business had occupied less than one hour.

CHAPTER EIGHT

To the victor. the spoils

ADMIRAL LORD EXMOUTH arrived in London on October 9, 1816. His reception, by the politicians, by his brother officers, by the newspapers, and by the public at large, was ecstatic. Honours and rewards were heaped upon him to an almost excessive degree. The Prince Regent raised him to the dignity of a Viscount. He was already a Knight Grand Cross of the Most Honourable Military Order of the Bath, but to this was now added a deluge of further distinctions: Knight of the Spanish Order of King Charles III, Knight Grand Cross of the Order of St Ferdinand and of Merit of Naples, Knight Grand Cross of the Military Order of Wilhelm of the Netherlands, Knight of the Royal Sardinian Military Order of St Maurice and St Lazarus, and Knight of the Sardinian Order of Annunciation.

The honours and tokens of esteem continued to be conferred upon Exmouth and his senior officers throughout the months after their return to England. They were national figures and public interest in the story of their expedition was immense. All of this must have been exceptionally galling to the man who obviously felt that he had been cheated of the chance to win glory, Vice Admiral Sir Charles Vinicombe Penrose.

Penrose, like Exmouth, was a Cornishman. Born at Gluvias, the son of a vicar, he entered the Royal Navy in 1771 at the relatively late age of sixteen and subsequently spent most of his life at sea. In 1776, as a midshipman in HMS *Levant*, he made his first visit to Algiers where he had the duty of escorting ashore five Algerine seamen who had been held previously at Malta as slaves of the Knights of St John. Later services in the Atlantic, West Indies and North Sea enabled him to distinguish himself and to

After the battle Lord Exmouth returned to Teignmouth. The town was a haven for former naval officers and one of these was Thomas Luny, the sailor-artist who specialised in maritime scenes. He was commissioned by the Admiral to paint a series of pictures and the two men met frequently. This canvas was one of Luny's interpretations of Exmouth's eye-witness account. It shows (extreme left) HMS Queen Charlotte, (left foreground) burning Algerine vessels, (centre foreground) the mole battery, (right foreground) the Dey defiantly waving his scimitar, (upper right) the Citadel, and (upper centre) the dome of the Dey's palace (by kind permission of Viscount Exmouth)

steadily climb the ladder of promotion. The price of success was indifferent health. Never a robust man, he suffered sunstroke in the West Indies and contracted severe rheumatism during the blockade of the Thirteen Colonies. His occasional periods ashore were spent convalescing on the family farm at Ethy, near Lostwithiel, in Cornwall.

In 1810 he was made commodore, flag officer commanding, at Gibraltar. Further promotion followed when he was appointed admiral in charge of all naval arrangements for Wellington's army in the Peninsula, an early example of the 'combined operations' role. Penrose did so well in this post, particularly at the bridging of the River Adour, that Wellington ordered him to take command of the Gironde area after the surrender of Napoleon.

Returning to England he was offered the appointment of flag officer commanding and commander-in-chief designate,

Mediterranean. Although he was not in good health, and although he had already more than forty years' service behind him, Penrose accepted. He sailed to the Mediterranean and replaced the Commander-in-Chief, Admiral Hallowell. A few months later Napoleon escaped from Elba. Europe was once again in turmoil. No official blame was attached to Penrose for failing to prevent the escape. However, the vacant post of Commander-in-Chief eluded him. Instead, on March 24, 1815, Lord Exmouth was reappointed C-in-C, having already acted in that capacity in 1811 and 1812. Penrose now became Exmouth's second-in-command and he must have had deep feelings of disappointment.

Exmouth and Penrose worked well together during the Hundred Days of Napoleon's return to power. Waterloo was fought and won, Napoleon departed for St Helena and Europe returned to the game of conferences and cartography. The prime reason for Exmouth's reappointment had been removed but, instead of immediately relinquishing command, he passed the winter at Leghorn and planned the undertaking given to him by the Admiralty, namely, the negotiation of a new treaty with each of the three Barbary states.

In the spring of 1816 Exmouth sailed to Algiers, Tunis and Tripoli, his flagship being the *Boyne*. Penrose sailed from Malta in his own flagship, *Bombay*, and together the two admirals cruised to each of the three ports. As we have already seen, those two earlier visits to Algiers (in April and May) failed to achieve anything of lasting value.

In May, 1816, Exmouth sailed for England, hauling down his flag as Commander-in-Chief, Mediterranean, and leaving Penrose in charge as flag officer commanding, as he had been before the Napoleon and Barbary missions. Penrose awaited the arrival of a signal confirming the appointment as C-in-C which had been promised to him prior to Napoleon's escape. It never came. In fact, he heard nothing from London other than a vaguely-worded despatch dated July 16, from the First Lord of the Admiralty, Lord Melville, to the effect that something was afoot. Penrose was soon all too aware of the fact that great events were astir and that they would involve his own area of responsibility. Like most people in France, Italy, or Malta, he heard rumours and saw newspaper reports to the effect that a powerful expedition was being mounted in England with the object of chastising the Algerines. Day after day he waited anxiously at Malta, but no word came. Finally, on August 19, he boarded the *Ister* and sailed west to Algiers, arriving there on the day after the battle.

Penrose cannot have reasonably expected to be given command of the expedition. Exmouth was his senior in rank, in experience, in fame and in ability. But he was fully justified in assuming that Lord Melville would place him under Exmouth as second-in-command or, at the very least, and as a matter of common courtesy, have given him some explanation.

On August 30, interspersed with his numerous meetings with the Dey, Penrose found time to pour out his frustration in a letter to J W Croker, First Secretary of the Admiralty,

'Sir, I must request you to inform their Lordships that, having for a considerable time seen accounts in the foreign newspapers that a large armament was coming into these seas, my anxiety was too great to wait longer for the official account I eagerly longed for and, on the 19th instant, I embarked on HMS *Ister*, leaving Captain Spencer of the *Erne* in charge at Malta, and proceeded in hopes of offering my services to Lord Exmouth in good time. I had (I think naturally) concluded that some dispatches had been sent to me, and lost, for I could never allow myself to believe that so heavy and irretrievable a mortification as I now acutely experience could be intended. At the end of forty-five years' faithful service to my King and country, I could never have expected, as I am conscious I have never merited, to have a junior officer from a distant station sent to second Lord Exmouth, on a service to be performed on that station where I commanded in chief, and that service never intimated to me in the smallest degree. I have the honour to be (etc).'

This letter, a *cri de coeur* if ever there was one, goes directly to the crux of the matter. Why was Admiral Milne, junior to Penrose, given the plum job of second-in-command to Exmouth? Milne, unlike Penrose, had never seen service in the Mediterranean and had no experience or qualification in dealing with the Barbary States. Most of his professional life had been spent in the Americas, the West Indies, the Indian Ocean and in home waters. During 1803 to 1811, the critical years of the war with Napoleon, he was a post captain commanding the Sea Fencibles (an early form of militia or Home Guard) in the Firth of Forth district. A mediocre officer, with limited sea and combat experience, he was a poor choice for the job and his mishandling of *Impregnable* during the battle exposed his deficiencies in leadership and seamanship. These shortcomings were aggravated by the fact that his flag captain, Edward Brace, was a sick old man long past his prime.

There is evidence to suggest that Milne lost his composure when faced with the appalling carnage in *Impregnable*. His signal to Exmouth, reporting the internal explosion and requesting assistance, assured his leader that 'although the *Impregnable* might sink, she would never surrender'. While admirably brave, such a statement has an oddly theatrical, almost hysterical, undertone. *Impregnable* was anchored five hundred yards from the shore and at no time was there the remotest possibility that the Algerines might make an attempt at boarding her.

We must assume that Milne had influence in Whitehall which Penrose did not. Whatever the explanation, Milne failed to distinguish himself in any way before, during or after the battle of Algiers and yet he was honoured lavishly, becoming a Knight Commander of the Bath, a Companion of the Order of Wilhelm of the Netherlands, and Knight of the Neapolitan Order of St Januarius.

Penrose, on the other hand, received a very cool response to his letter of complaint, so cool in fact that he felt obliged to write subsequently a letter of apology for his previous outspokenness. He worked hard for Exmouth at Algiers, taking charge of most of the negotiations with the Dey and his officers. While many other officers connected with the expedition received handsome recognition and reward, the unfortunate Penrose was ignored.

There is nothing in Penrose's record to show that he had any active enemies in high places or that he had ever failed in his duty. It is therefore improbable that he was excluded intentionally from the Algiers venture. The most likely explanation is that Exmouth was chosen to lead because he was the obvious choice and would in any event have insisted upon being given the opportunity to protect his reputation. As far as the post of second-in-command is concerned, the exclusion of Penrose reflects nothing more significant than the great speed with which the expedition was mounted. There simply was no opportunity to send long and detailed despatches out to Malta; the time factor did not permit prolonged and careful co-ordination of Exmouth's squadron with Penrose's force. Milne secured the job because he asked for it and he happened to be available in Plymouth in July (aboard HMS *Leander*).

That Exmouth was aware of Penrose's anguish, and sympathised with it, is a fact demonstrated by the following entry, dated August 31, in Admiral Penrose's journal,

'Little did I expect to be employed in any part of a business with the main struggle of which I had unfortunately no participation; but Lord Exmouth, calling me to a private audience, with a considerable degree of embarrassment, asked me, as a mark of friendship towards him, if I would undertake to arrange the treaty, the remaining business with the Dey. Neither private nor public considerations allowed me to hesitate, though no proposal could have come more unexpected; and within the hour or two I was standing before my old acquaintance the Dey.'

After Algiers, and the departure of Exmouth, Admiral Penrose remained in the Mediterranean and acted as Commander-in-Chief for the next three years. He retired to Ethy in 1819 where he lived quietly, and forgotten by the world, until his death in 1829.

Admiral Sir Sidney Smith was another senior officer who expressed resentment at the Admiralty's decision to appoint Exmouth as leader of the expedition (but with far less justification than in the case of Penrose). Smith became increasingly cantankerous and eccentric in his later years. It was his publicity campaign which had focussed attention on the Christian slavery scandal and he therefore believed that he had the right to be given command of the attack. He was profoundly irritated when the task was given to his former Commander-in-Chief. For reasons best known to himself, he decided to express his disapproval to the King of France. His request for a private audience was finally granted, after a delay of many weeks, and Smith launched into a long tirade. The substance of his speech soon became common knowledge and the Duke of Wellington, who regarded Smith as 'a silly man, a mere vaporizer', gleefully recounted the scene on numerous later occasions. According to the Duke's version, Smith stood before the King and said that it was 'his business to acquaint His Majesty that the expedition must fail; that the force was insufficient and bad of its kind; but above all that the commander was ill-selected; that he knew Lord Exmouth well, having served with him, and that whatever qualities he might have as a mere sailor, he was the most unfit man in all other respects to command such an enterprise; that he himself was, from a variety of considerations, the only person who ought to have been selected; and, finally, by this omission, an affair so vitally important to the civilised world must, to an absolute and demonstrative certainty, fail.'

The Duke of Wellington's story continued, 'Louis XVIII was a sly old man with a quiet sense of humour. He listened to Smith without interruption and, when he had concluded his very long speech, he told Sir Sidney that he was very much obliged to him, for the information that he was so good as to give him, that he quite appreciated his motives, but, he added, I am sure it will give you additional pleasure, as it has done to me since I heard your opinion, to learn that we have this morning heard, through Marseilles, that what you fear is impracticable has been accomplished with the most complete success!'

Sir Sidney Smith's reputation was badly battered when details of this interview were gossiped through the *salons* of Paris and London. Despite all his earlier efforts it was Exmouth who was the shining hero of Algiers, who was scooping up all the prizes, while he himself had become a figure of fun. Smith went into decline and never received the recognition which he truly deserved.

Not for the first time, and certainly not for the last, the distribution of honours and awards became a bone of contention for the officers who had distinguished themselves at Algiers. Some were favoured, others were not, and there is no discernible pattern to the method of their selection. Certainly those officers who had fought aboard *Queen Charlotte*, or had been personally observed by Admiral Lord Exmouth during the battle, stood a better chance of reward than their contemporaries in other ships (fighting with equal valour but hidden by the smoke).

There were five naval officers who particularly distinguished themselves at Algiers. The treatment which they received subsequently from Exmouth and the Admiralty neatly illustrates the unfairness of the system. Their varying fortunes also reflect the limited career prospects facing naval officers as Great Britain entered the era of the Forty Years Peace.

Lieutenant Peter Richards commanded the gallant and successful attack on the Algerine blockship. His reward came within three weeks when he was promoted to the rank of commander. He continued his career in the service, attained post rank in 1828 and served with great distinction in the Opium War in China (1840-1842).

Lieutenant Richard Fleming commanded the battering vessel *Invincible* during the early hours of the bombardment. Moored under the flagship's stern, armed with a 68-pounder carronade and a 24-pounder, this flat-boat went on firing until her ammunition was used up. Fleming then took command of the explosion vessel *Fly*, a 'hazardous duty' by any standard. He was promoted commander and admitted to the Royal Sardinian Military Order of St Maurice and St Lazarus. He also received a commemmorative medallion from Sir Sidney Smith's 'Knights Liberator' organisation in Paris. The glory and acclaim soon turned sour when he was put on half-pay and received no further employment for the next thirty years!

Master John Gaze played the part of confidante and right hand man to Lord Exmouth, the role he had filled on numerous other occasions during their twenty-three years of almost continuous service together. As Master of the Fleet, he was the admiral's closest advisor on all matters relating to seamanship and navigation. His rank was still that of master, but his responsibilities were vastly greater than those carried by any other officer of such comparatively modest rank in the Royal Navy. It is certain that Exmouth did not settle upon his final plan of battle without first consulting John Gaze. It is equally sure that Gaze had a guiding influence upon the safe navigation of the squadron from England to Algiers Bay and the conning of *Queen Charlotte* to her anchorage by the mole. That final approach, gently nursing the 2,300 tons of *Queen Charlotte's* dead weight to within fifty yards of the enemy, with a dying breeze and the ship almost aground, called for the most delicate judgement. One small mistake could have brought ruin. It is therefore baffling to find that Master Gaze went unrewarded for his services, receiving neither promotion nor recognition. In October 1816 he was given the job of assistant to the Master Attendant at Plymouth Dockyard and a year later Lord Exmouth arranged for him to be appointed master aboard *Impregnable*. Four years later he became Master Attendant at Portsmouth and later filled the same office at Sheerness. He eventually received his promotion to the rank of commander when he retired, in 1846, at the age of seventy four!

Captain William Dashwood carried far more direct personal responsibility than any other officer of such junior rank during the weeks preceding the battle. He had joined the Royal Navy in 1799 when still a child of nine. He fought at Copenhagen and served with Exmouth aboard *Culloden* in the East Indies. In 1811 his right arm was shot off during the action with the French frigate *La Pomone*. At the time of Algiers he was twenty-six years of age, the commander in command of a fine little ship which he had commissioned when new from the builders. *Prometheus* was his pride and joy. Her value lay in the fact that she was 'eyes and ears' to Exmouth prior to the admiral's arrival in late August. Dashwood's attempted rescue of Consul McDonell and his family revealed mature judgement and a strong sense of

initiative. He was obviously an excellent young man, but he received no reward or mark of distinction for his services. He was promoted post captain two years later and then placed on half pay. At twenty-eight his career was finished.

Captain Charles Warde was another officer who made a vital contribution to the success of the expedition. His secret mission to survey the port and its defences provided the basis for Exmouth's plan of battle. The slightest negligence on his part could have been ruinous, particularly if his report had been inaccurate regarding the depth of water by the mole and port entrance. An error of only two or three feet would have put *Queen Charlotte* hard aground and helpless. It is quite extraordinary, therefore, that he received no recognition and no further employment. Despite the fact that he had been selected personally by Exmouth to make the survey, and despite the fact that Exmouth had earlier selected him as part of his retinue when the admiral visited Rome on a diplomatic mission in 1815, Charles Warde seems to have been abandoned by his chief when the squadron returned to England. He did enjoy some small compensation twenty years later when one of his old captains, Sir Edward Owen, persuaded King William IV to make him a Knight of the Royal Guelphic Order 'in recognition of his services at Algiers'. Apart from this belated token, Captain Charles Warde was just one more forgotten hero. There were many others.

Admiral Lord Exmouth, for his part, could not have been forgotten by the public even if he had so wished. The government had, at long last, a triumph with which to answer its critics at home and abroad. The pressure exerted previously by the Congress of Vienna was removed at a stroke. The embarrassment caused by Exmouth's earlier visit to Barbary was entirely dispersed. The political and propaganda value of the victory was substantial and the authorities squeezed it for every possible drop of advantage to themselves.

The House of Commons joined the fanfare with a formal and unanimous Vote of Thanks,

'Thanks to Admiral Lord Viscount Exmouth, and other Officers, for their gallant conduct in the decisive Attack on the Batteries and Naval Force of Algiers. House of Commons, Monday, 3rd of February, 1817.

Resolved, *nemine contradicente,* that the thanks of this House be given to Admiral Lord Viscount Exmouth, Knight Grand Cross of the Most Honourable Military Order of the Bath, for his able and gallant conduct in the successful and decisive attack on the Batteries and Naval Force of Algiers on the 27th August, 1816.

Resolved, *nemine contradicente,* that the thanks of this house be given to Rear Admiral Sir David Milne, Knight Commander of the Most Honourable Military Order of the Bath, and to the several Captains and Officers of the Fleet employed on that memorable occasion.

Resolved, *nemine contradicente,* that this House doth acknowledge and highly approve the Services of the Seamen and Royal Marines serving in the Fleet before Algiers, on the 27th August, 1816.

Resolved, *nemine contradicente,* that the thanks of this House be given to Vice-Admiral Baron van Capellen, and the Naval Forces of His Majesty the King of the Netherlands under the

Designed by the famous silversmith Paul Storr, this spectacular
table centre was presented to Exmouth by his officers in 1817.
It features the Algiers lighthouse battery, with the figures of a
British sailor striking down a Corsair and a naval officer freeing
a grateful slave (National Maritime Museum)

Vice-Admiral's command, for their cordial assistance and co-
operation in the Attack on Algiers, on the 27th August, 1816.

Ordered, that Mr Speaker do communicate the said
Resolutions to Admiral Lord Viscount Exmouth, and that his
Lordship be requested to make known the same to the several
Officers under his Lordship's command, and in co-operation
with His Majesty's Navy in the said Service.'

A similar vote of thanks was approved by the Commons two
days later in respect of the Royal Engineers, Royal Sappers &
Miners, and Royal Horse Artillery, who had served at Algiers. In
parallel with the votes conveyed by the Commons, similar
resolutions were approved by the House of Lords.

The last occasion when Westminster had passed resolutions of
this nature had been the votes of thanks addressed to the Duke of
Wellington for his service at the battle of Waterloo. Further token
of the importance attached to Exmouth's expedition was the
relative rarity of these votes of thanks. As precedent we have,

amongst others, the examples of Parker and Nelson (1801) for Copenhagen; Saumarez (1801) for Gibraltar; Wellesley, Clive and Lake (1804) for India; Gambier (1810) for Basque Roads; and Wellington (1814) at the conclusion of the war with France.

In addition to the approval of the politicians, there was the recognition of his achievement by the Prince Regent to be enjoyed. By order of the Prince a large gold medallion was struck and presented to Exmouth in commemoration of his victory. On the obverse was the bust of the Prince and the legend, *To tame the proud, the fetter'd slave to free. These are imperial arts and worthy thee.* Below came the words, *George Prince Regent.* On the reverse of the medallion was a representation of the battle and, in the exergue, the words, *Algiers bombarded its fleet destroyed and Christian slavery extinguished, August 27th 1816.* Four examples of this medal were struck; we are not told who received the other three.

The Dutch contribution to the battle was fully acknowledged. Apart from being individually named in Parliament's vote of thanks (the first time such an honour had ever been bestowed upon a non-British naval commander), Admiral van Capellen was made a Commander of the Bath by the Prince Regent and presented with a sword of honour by the Duke of Clarence. These honours recognised not only the Dutchman's professional skill and personal courage, but also the fact that he had been acting entirely on his own initiative when he had volunteered to join forces with the British on August 9. He had sent a letter to The Hague several days earlier — asking for official approval — but it was obvious that he and Exmouth would have made their own decisions long before a reply could be expected. In the event, a favourable reply did reach Gibraltar in September, several days after the Dutch squadron had returned from the bombardment. It was fortunate for the safety of Admiral van Capellen's future pension that his suggestion was approved by the Dutch authorities!

The British public followed the example set by its royal and parliamentary leaders. There was a spate of literary and artistic acclaim. An extraordinary amount of poetry was published, much of it of indifferent quality, praising Exmouth's skills and his Christian ideals.

'Here, Exmouth, rest! thou bravest, gentlest mind,
Thy country's friend, but more of human kind;

Standing three feet in height, this magnificent piece
of silver was presented to the Admiral by the city of
Marseilles 'in testimony of its gratitude'. Made by Charles
Cahier, silversmith to the King of France, it was one
of the few tokens of recognition to come from England's
recently defeated enemy (photo by Christies, by kind
permission of Viscount Exmouth)

Thou born to arms, thy worth in youth approv'd,
In age still better known, and more belov'd!
From war, awhile retire, yet not far hence remove
Thy martial spirit, or thy social love,
For thee the hardy veteran still would drop a tear,
And the gay courtier ever heave the sigh sincere.'

Several popular ballads were published, and presumably
performed, for the diversion of the British people. Enterprising
promoters toured the country with instructional displays, some
in diorama form, and the crowds flocked to see these
entertainments. With no further battles or campaigns to capture
public imagination and enthusiasm, the story continued to
generate a profit for the showmen and publishers for several
years after the battle. It became, in effect, something of a cult. As
late as 1825 a new opera in three acts, *The fall of Algiers*, was
performed in London. In 1830 a Christmas play, *The battle of
Algiers*, a one act play in verse, was published in Devonport.

Old sailors could earn a tankard of ale or a nip of rum by
visiting public houses and telling the tale of their heroic
adventures under Exmouth's command. One of these men,
William Nelson, earned a respectable living by having his alleged
experiences 'ghosted' by a professional writer. The story was
printed as a tract and William hawked his pamphlets around the
market places of Lancashire at the price of one penny each. He
was a negro, apparently a Lancastrian, who claimed to have
served as personal servant to Horatio Nelson from 1790 to 1805.
Nelson converted him to Christianity, he said, and gave him his
surname. After Trafalgar and the death of his master, William
had served Admiral Lord Collingwood before leaving the Royal
Navy and joining the merchant service. Then, the tale went on,
he had been captured by Algerine Corsairs and enslaved for four
years until liberated by Admiral Lord Exmouth in 1816. His

One of Exmouth's many rewards was the granting of a viscountancy. This elevation of his degree of nobility entailed a long correspondence with the College of Arms. The Admiral followed the contemporary fashion by asking the heralds to augment his armorial bearings with those episodes in his career of which he was most proud. The lion rests his paw on the defeated crescent of Islam. A liberated slave holds the cross of Christ in one hand, his broken fetters in the other. In the centre, Algiers and HMS Queen Charlotte. Above, a representation of Plymouth Citadel and the wreck of the Dutton. The Latin motto signifies 'God being my helper'

descriptions of the tortures inflicted upon his fellow slaves were so lurid and disgusting that a ready sale for his tracts was guaranteed for many years. He is known to have been enjoying brisk sales in Wakefield market as late as 1830. It is perhaps rather sad to find that, although William undoubtedly saw much service in HMS *Victory* and other ships, his yarn does not survive close investigation. He was a splendid liar. The buying public probably did not really care whether or not his tracts were factually correct, they simply wanted to satisfy their continuing interest in Exmouth's celebrated victory.

Exmouth, for his part, did not feel the urge of authorship. He was famous and he was wealthy. He could afford to rest on his laurels and enjoy the applause. He received the freedom of several towns and cities. He attended many formal dinners as the principal guest, one of these being given by the aldermen of the City of London who presented him with a sword, a laudatory speech being made by the Lord Mayor.

He attended a banquet prepared for him by the Ironmongers'

Company who happened to be the trustees of an estate of £2,000 per annum bequeathed many years earlier by one of their members, a Mr Bretton. This gentleman had at one time been taken prisoner by the Corsairs and his bequest was intended for the ransom of British captives of the Barbary states. The Ironmongers maintained their own agent in Barbary for this very purpose.

One year after the battle, Admiral Lord Exmouth was guest of honour at a banquet given by the officers who had served under him at Algiers. They presented him with a silver table centre, a piece of plate 'of massy size and elegant workmanship, as a mark of their admiration for his conduct'. It was made by Rundell & Company of London and cost one thousand and four hundred guineas.

Exmouth had never been a truly popular figure, either in the public's mind or in the eyes of his fellow officers. It is true that he enjoyed great local affection in Plymouth and Falmouth, but perhaps he was not by his nature a lovable man. After Algiers he came as close to national adulation as circumstance and the limitations of his character could permit. Later commentators were to compare his qualities with those of Nelson. While Exmouth was certainly an outstanding seaman and organiser, equally surely he did not possess the genius of Nelson. However, the fact that such comparison should be made at all is a fair measure of the standing which he achieved after his return from Barbary. For the next three years he served as port admiral at Plymouth and then retired at the age of sixty-three. He never again served in a sea-going capacity. During the following years he continued to receive a variety of honours from cities and universities. His final official honour, a sinecure, was to be made Vice-Admiral of Great Britain. He died on January 23, 1833, at the age of 76, and was buried in the family vault at St James' Parish Church, Christow, near Exeter. He had given instructions that the funeral should be a quiet family affair and that his coffin should be borne into the church, not by a naval party, but by ten labourers from the Canonteign estate. He even declined to have his name commemorated, as is the custom, in the crypt of St Paul's Cathedral. Despite his wishes, news of his death was widely reported and there was a large congregation of Devonshire gentry at the funeral service. Several of his old captains made long journeys to salute their former chief. Among them, from the Algiers expedition, were Ekins of the *Superb*, Paterson of the *Minden*, and Aylmer of the *Severn*.

He had had a long and successful career. In the words of the present Lord Exmouth, 'He was always a lucky man. He was brilliant, of course, but luck played a large part. He was always in the right place at the right time. And time and again he placed himself in positions of danger but was never seriously hurt. When you look at what happened to Nelson and some of their contemporaries, the admiral had almost a charmed life'.

Unlike the admiral himself, many of those who sailed with him to Algiers were fated not to see England again. The chances of war denied them the dignity of growing old gracefully. The sailors killed in the battle, or who died in the following weeks, were quickly forgotten by all but their own families. Small pensions were available for mutilated survivors and for the widows of those who did not return, but official funds offered poor recompense for the loss of the family breadwinner. Charity was an important source of financial support for the dependents.

The following letter, dated December 28, 1816, was signed by the captain and crew of a ship anchored at Spithead and was addressed to J W Croker, Secretary at the Admiralty,

'We the Captain, Officers and Ship's Company of His Majesty's Ship *Tyne*, being of the few of late who have been making Prize

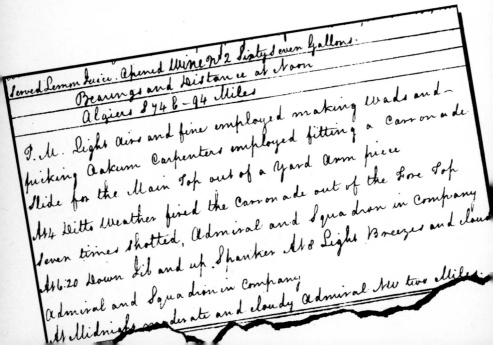

Money, do request you to submit to the Lords Commissioner of the Admiralty our desire for subscribing a fortnight's pay for the relief of the Widows and Orphans of the Petty Officers and Seamen who fell in the British Fleet under the command of Lord Exmouth off Algiers.'

Within three days they received Croker's ice-cold reply,

'Acquaint them that there being no fund created for this purpose, nor means of dividing their contributions, Their Lordships do not think it proper to comply with their request.'

There was, it would seem, a profound difference between the value of one victorious live admiral and the value of the hundred and more sailors who had died for that victory.

In fairness to Exmouth it must be recorded that he did at least try to persuade the British government to issue a distinctive medal to all the officers and men who had participated in the battle. He made an approach to John Croker with this suggestion but, despite the strong bond of friendship between the two, he was firmly turned down. Croker wrote to the Admiral on October 23, 1816,

'My dear Lord,
I never have and never will (I hope) do anything for the sake of popularity; he that steers by any other compass than his own sense of duty may be a popular, but cannot be an honest, and I think not a useful public servant. On the occasion of a medal for the Algerine exploit I have no hesitation in telling you that I decidedly disapprove of it; and if my opinion were asked (which it has not been) I should say so. Why should that be done for 5,000 men who were at Algiers, which has not been done for the millions of men who have served in so many glorious actions since 1793? You will say that the soldiers of Waterloo have had medals, but surely it is impossible to compare Waterloo with any other battle. The soldiers of Salamanca, Talavera, Vittoria, Toulouse and the Pyrenees, have no medals. In short, my dear Lord, with the justest sense of the skill and gallantry of your operations before Algiers, and of the admirable courage displayed by all ranks, and the wonderful success of your fire, I must say that I should be sorry to see anything done for it, which

173

should seem to throw a shade over the 1st June, Camperdown, St Vincent's, the Nile and Trafalgar.

Yours, etc, J W Croker

Looking back at those events of the early nineteenth century, studying the flow of powerful emotions which they aroused, it is hard to understand why the battle of Algiers has been largely forgotten. Every English schoolboy acquires at least a superficial knowledge of the great battles listed in his history books. Hastings, Agincourt, Culloden, Trafalgar, Waterloo, Balaclava, Omdurman, these have the stuff which captures the imagination. The basic details of how and why these actions were fought remain in the mind. Similarly, the story of the anti-slavery campaign is at least vaguely familiar to the average student of history. The name of Wilberforce lurks not too far down the well of memory. But the story of Exmouth's triumph has somehow lost the aura which surrounded it in the years immediately following its achievement. Even to the specialist student of naval history this is not a familiar battle.

Unlike Trafalgar, the battle of Algiers did not cause the death of a great national hero. Unlike the Spanish Armada, the action did not take place within sight of our own shores. Unlike Acre or Aboukir Bay, it did not frustrate the expansion of an empire. Despite contemporary claims, it did not even wipe out Christian slavery and the Corsairs. It does deserve, however, a prominent place in any list of important exercises in British maritime power.

Apart from its obvious dramatic and heroic content, the story illustrates with dreadful clarity the futility of sending brave and skilful soldiers and sailors to fight battles which have been inadequately considered by their superiors and by their political masters.

The failure of one expedition after another proved beyond doubt that nothing could be gained by bombardment alone; permanent occupation was the only lasting solution. Before 1829 no government was ever prepared to grasp the nettle. There was a fatal misconception by the British regarding the military nature of the problem. Algiers was viewed as being a maritime state having the ability to damage Britain's trade routes. The solution was therefore judged to be a matter solely for the Royal Navy. It was the navy which was sent back time and again to subdue the Deys. It was the navy which was expected to charge bull-like at the massive seaward defences of the port. It was the Admiralty which accepted this task without ever once stopping to consider whether or not this was the most intelligent course. Hind-sight suggests in fact that neither the strategy nor the tactics had any merit whatsoever. In strategic terms it should have been plain that occasional punitive raids could not alter the mentality of an entire population. The Algerines were committed by religion, custom and heredity to see life from a particular viewpoint. Destroy their ships and they would steal or buy a replacement fleet. Kill their soldiers and they could recruit a new army. Knock down their houses and they would seize more slaves to carry out the work of reconstruction. Kill one Dey and they could elect a new one. It was the overall system which needed to be destroyed, not the outward vestments of that system. Such a radical change could be achieved only by total conquest and permanent occupation.

The fact that the port was guarded by some of the most formidable armaments in the world seemed to call for nothing more than larger ships, larger fleets and heavier shot. Each British expedition arrived directly by sea and placed itself immediately in the line of sight of the powerful coastal batteries. Whether they came bearing olive-branches or threats, gifts or menaces, the British admirals automatically forfeited all chance of success the moment they dropped anchor in the bay. It is hardly surprising that their attempts at diplomacy were doomed to failure, with their ships in shallow water on a dangerous shore and exposed to the threat of a thousand cannon. The arrogant and audacious behaviour of the Deys must be surely attributed to the poor bargaining position in which the admirals repeatedly placed themselves. Great Britain would have rid herself of the burden many years earlier if a general had been given the task instead of an admiral. The landward defences of Algiers were relatively weak and invited precisely the type of enveloping attack finally adopted by the French in 1829. The suppression of Christian slavery was always, in the final analysis, a job which needed to be done by soldiers rather than by sailors or diplomats.

Indeed, 1816 would have been the ideal year for such a venture. Wellington's army of occupation had plenty of seasoned regiments stationed throughout France and available for employment. Having fought its way across Spain and over the Pyrenees, having beseiged and stormed several strongly fortified cities in the process, the British army was eminently qualified to tackle Algiers. Once ashore, the battle-hardened veterans of the Peninsula would have made mince-meat of Omar Bashaw's men. The Algerines had never been obliged to fight a conventional land battle. They had neither the experience nor the equipment for anything more than token resistance to a military invasion.

There would have been great difficulties in the way of a major military expedition, the most obvious being the immediate lack of manned ships to carry the troops and their impedimenta to North Africa from France or England. The financial cost would have been much higher. It would all have taken much longer to organise. It might have been necessary to delay the expedition until the spring of 1817, and this would have meant another six or eight months of diplomatic harrassment for Lord Castlereagh and his colleagues in the British government.

Lord Exmouth's expedition was mounted in a hurry and it was an act of short-term political expediency. It was a response by the British government to its critics at Westminster and in Europe. The one man who had the fire-power to do the job thoroughly was the Duke of Wellington, lustily enjoying the fruits of victory in Paris, but he was never consulted.

None of this detracts from the quality of the glory won by Exmouth and by the officers and men who sailed with him. British and Dutch alike, they achieved an astonishing success against a brave and powerful adversary and could claim with pride to have done their duty.

Appendices

A DIARY OF EVENTS

SOME IMPORTANT DATES in the rise and fall of the Corsairs of Algiers, with particular reference to the role of the Royal Navy.

1529 — Barbarossa fortifies the harbour and creates a Corsair fleet

1541 — a powerful international force, commanded by Emperor Charles V, lands and destroys the city. The Algerines rebuild it

1581 — Queen Elizabeth appoints an ambassador and formal trade relations are established with England

England gives full recognition that Algiers is a sovereign state, hence the letters of marque carried by the Corsairs protect them from the charge of piracy

1602 — Queen Elizabeth writes to the Dey, complaining of the seizure of English ships and cargoes

1620 — King James I sends a squadron of 18 ships from Plymouth under the command of Sir Robert Mansel. He threatens to bombard the city, fails to do so and returns home empty-handed

1621 — the Corsairs capture 40 English ships in less than a year. King James I sends Sir Thomas Roe to Algiers to make a new treaty

1623 — England places an embargo on the export of munitions to Algiers. There is much fruitless debate regarding possible solutions to the Algiers problem

1631 — the British Consul reports that 25,000 Christians are captive and held in wretched conditions. Among them, the entire population of Baltimore, a small Irish fishing village, seized on June 31 of that year

1640 — Corsairs cruise off Exeter, Plymouth, Dartmouth and Barnstaple, seizing many English merchantmen. They land near Penzance and carry off 60 villagers. Parliament responds by raising a tax for the redemption of hostages from Algiers

1654 — Oliver Cromwell sends a squadron commanded by Admiral Robert Blake who imposes a new treaty 'which shall endure to the end of time and which can be broken by no man'

1660 — King Charles II sends a squadron commanded by Lord Sandwich to implement the previous treaty. The English fire on the city but cause little damage

1664 — Captain Nicholas Parker of HMS *Nonsuch* is appointed consul, the first time the Royal Navy has become directly involved in Algerine affairs

1668 — Sir Thomas Allen arrives with nine warships and two fireships. His threats result in the freeing of many English slaves

1669 — Samuel Pepys convinces Charles II that the current treaty is humiliating to England. Sir Thomas Allen returns with a larger fleet, exchanges cannon-fire with the defences and sails away again. The expedition is a total failure

1670 — Sir Thomas Allen makes a third visit to the Mediterranean and combines with a Dutch squadron under Admiral van Ghent (thus creating an interesting precedent for Lord Exmouth's expedition in 1816). They sink six Corsairs at sea. Some of Allen's ships, led by Sir Edward Spragg, attack Algiers and drive headlong into the port area. They sink many Algerine vessels, set fire to the harbour installations and cause heavy damage in the city. Within months the Algerines rebuild the defences, re-equip their fleet and recommence raiding

1674 — Sir John Narborough arrives with a small squadron and redeems 189 English slaves at a cost of 62,300 pieces of eight

1676 — Corsairs capture the Royal Navy ketch *Quaker*. The English are humiliated during the attempts to recover her

1681 — Admiral the Hon Arthur Herbert attempts to suppress the Corsairs but is obliged to renew the old treaty (which still leaves the Algerines with the right to stop and search English ships on the high seas)

1682 — a French squadron commanded by Admiral the Marquis Duquesne twice bombards the city, firing 6,000 explosive shells and killing 800 persons. The Dey retaliates by blowing captives from the mouth of a cannon

1688 — the French renew their war and send 20 warships under Marshal Duc d'Estrées to bombard the city. They launch 13,300 mortar bombs in ten days and destroy much of the residential area, but fail to suppress the batteries. The English exploit the animosity between France and Algiers by improving their own diplomatic and commercial position in the area

1689 — William and Mary send messages of friendship to the Dey. The Corsairs continue to seize English ships

1694 — Sir Francis Wheeler sails for the Mediterranean to impress the Barbary states with the power of the Royal Navy. All but three of his fourteen warships are lost in a storm. British prestige suffers accordingly

1699 — Vice-Admiral Aylmer arrives with his squadron and signs a new treaty

1703 — Admiral George Byng arrives with another squadron and signs yet another treaty. The Algerines continue to seize English ships and crews

1722 — Corsairs seize a Quaker ship sailing from Plymouth to America. George Fox writes to the Dey, arguing that slavery is unlawful according to the Koran. Ship and crew are released without ransom

1739 — Admiral Haddock arrives with a squadron and delivers gifts and a message of goodwill from King George II. He demands the release of all English slaves but sails away empty-handed

1747 — Algerine Corsairs capture a ship carrying 77 officers and men of the Hibernian Regiment together with their wives and children. They are sold into slavery. No action is taken to recover them

1749 — Commodore the Hon Augustus Keppel attempts to recover an English vessel seized while carrying £25,000 sterling for the Postmaster General of Great Britain. He fails

1767 — Commodore Spry is humiliated during negotiations for the purchase of cattle and grain needed by the British garrisons on Minorca and Gibraltar

1784 — a Spanish admiral arrives with a fleet of 83 ships from Spain, Portugal, Naples and Malta. For several days they bombard the port from long range before sailing away. Damage is slight

1796 — the English are in sore need of allies in their fight against Napoleon. They curry favour with the Dey by bringing into Algiers ships which the Royal Navy has captured from the French. The French crews are sold into slavery

1801 — the British Consul, John Falcon, negotiates the release without ransom of 23 English ships and 266 crewman seized by Corsairs while attempting to supply the British forces on Malta

1803 — the United States declare war on the Barbary states. Commodore Edward

Preble imposes a treaty on Tripoli, but the Americans continue to pay tribute to Tunis and Algiers

1811 — the British government sends valuable gifts and assurances of friendship to the Dey. Supplies from Algiers are vital to Wellington's troops fighting in Spain

1812 — John McDonell, a professional soldier, is appointed British consul at Algiers. The British and Americans are distracted from the Corsair problem by their war against each other

1814 — the Congress of Vienna condemns Christian slavery and pressure is applied to the British to take action

1815 — the United States sign a lasting treaty. Captain Charles Warde is sent on a secret reconnaissance mission

1816 — Exmouth visits Algiers in April. He ransoms some Sardinian and Sicilian slaves and makes an agreement of doubtful value before sailing on to Tunis and Tripoli.

He returns in May and attempts to negotiate a better agreement. He quarrels with Omar Bashaw and John McDonell is arrested. Exmouth then returns to England with his squadron.

He is given command of an expeditionary force in July and returns to bombard Algiers in company with a Dutch force on August 27

1817 — most of the damage has been repaired. The Corsairs continue to attack the shipping of the Hanseatic League

1818 — Captain William F Wise, who commanded *Granicus* at the battle, returns in *Spartan* to register a protest at recent breaches of the treaty made with Exmouth

1818 — the Congress of Aix-la-Chappelle passes a resolution to suppress the Corsairs

1819 — an Anglo-French fleet arrives with a demand by the united European powers that the Algerines should finally renounce all forms of slavery. The Algerines man their defences and defy the two admirals, Julien and Freemantle, to attack them. The challenge is not accepted and the fleet sails away with nothing achieved

1823 — there is a marked escalation in Corsair activity

1824 — tension increases and there is a fierce sea battle between a Corsair and two ships of the Royal Navy. The French send a squadron of five warships to exert pressure on the Dey. The pressure is ignored and the Dey declares his intention to recommence Christian enslavement. He renounces all former treaties. Great Britain now declares herself to be at war with Algiers and two ships, HMS *Regent* and HMS *Naiad*, arrive under the command of Vice-Admiral Sir Harry Neale. He blockades the port. The American Consul, Shaler, tries to persuade the Dey that it would be foolhardy to risk another confrontation with the British government, but the Algerine remains defiant. Several more Royal Navy ships arrive, including the powerful HMS *Revenge*. On July 12 there is a general exchange of fire between the shore and the British squadron. Twelve days later the blockading fleet moves in closer to shore and commences a bombardment of the defences and the city. One of the Royal Navy ships is a steamer and her funnel is shot away. The Algerines send out several hundred pulling-boats armed with chasers and the British are obliged to keep their distance. Neale suspends the bombardment and reopens negotiations. Yet another treaty is signed, the terms being exactly what the Dey had been insisting upon before the arrival of Neale's squadron. The British depart, having failed completely to achieve their purpose

1829 — the French Consul grossly insults the Dey during a formal audience. Both men lose their tempers and strike each other.

Franco-Algerine relations deteriorate rapidly and some French sailors are massacred and decapitated. Their heads are used as footballs by the mob. Some weeks later two French naval brigs run ashore in thick fog and are wrecked. The

Dey's troops murder the 109 survivors and display their heads in Algiers. The Dey distributes a reward of $100 per head. French fury is aroused and a powerful military expedition is landed on the coast at Sidi Ferrudj. A French naval squadron supports this beach-head while another blockades the port of Algiers. A scratch force of Algerine soldiery attacks the French encampments, is beaten and scatters in panic into the hills. The French devote several days to landing stores, cavalry, artillery and a battering train. They then advance rapidly upon the city, sweeping aside any resistance, and begin firing at the landward city walls. The Dey surrenders the city and the campaign is over: the French have achieved in three weeks that which other nations had failed to achieve in three hundred years. The Dey and his entourage are shipped off to exile in Naples. His officers, administrators and mercenaries are similarly transported by the French Navy to Italy and the Levant. A Muslim cabinet is appointed under a French governor and Algiers becomes *de facto* a possession of the French Empire.

THE COMPOSITION OF THE ANGLO-DUTCH FLEET

The Ships of Admiral Lord Exmouth's Squadron

Queen Charlotte — *Captain James Brisbane CB*
First rate ship of the line armed with 104 guns. 3-decker. Built in oak at Deptford Royal Dockyard and launched May 17, 1810. Length 190ft, beam 53 ft, 2,289 bm tons. Renamed *Excellent* in December, 1859, and used as a gunnery training ship. Sold to J Read of Portsmouth in January, 1892, for breaking

Impregnable — *Captain Edward Brace CB*
Second rate ship of the line armed with 98 guns. 3-decker. Built in oak at Chatham Royal Dockyard and launched August 1, 1810. Her design was almost identical to that of HMS *Victory*. Length 197 ft, beam 53 ft, 2,406 bm tons. Draught 26 ft. Crew of 800 men.
Renamed *Kent* in November, 1888. Renamed *Caledonia* in September, 1891. Used as a boys' training ship under both names. Sold to Castle, in July, 1906, for breaking.

Superb — *Captain Charles Ekins**
Third rate ship of the line armed with 74 guns. 2-decker. Built in oak by Pitcher of Northfleet and launched March 19, 1798. Length 182 ft, beam 49 ft, 1,919 bm tons. Broken up, work completed in April 1826

Minden — *Captain William Paterson*
Third rate ship of the line armed with 74 guns. 2-decker. Built in teak at Bombay Royal Dockyard and launched June 19, 1810. Length 171 ft, beam 49 ft, 1,721 bm tons.
Converted for use as a hospital bulk in 1842. Sold to breakers at Hong Kong in July, 1861

Albion — *Captain John Coode**
Third rate ship of the line armed with 74 guns. 2-decker. Built in oak by Perry of Blackwall and launched June 17, 1802. Length 175 ft, beam 48 ft, 1,743 bm tons.
Converted to harbour service in July, 1831. Broken up at Deptford, work completed in June, 1836

Leander — *Captain Edward Chetham CB**
Fourth rate frigate armed with 58 guns. Built by Wigram & Green of Blackwall and launched November 10, 1813. Length 174 ft, beam 45 ft, 1,572 bm tons. Constructed in pitch-pine and carrying 26 x 42-pounder carronades and 32 x 24-pounder cannon. Broken up, work completed March, 1830

Severn — *Captain the Hon Frederick W Aylmer**
Fourth rate frigate armed with 50 guns. Built by Wigram & Green of Blackwall and launched June 14, 1813. Length 159 ft, beam 42 ft, 1,240 bm tons. Built in pitch-pine and carrying 20 x 32-pounder carronades and 28 x 24-pounder cannon. Sold to J Ledger for breaking in July, 1825

Glasgow — *Captain the Hon Anthony Maitland**
Fourth rate frigate armed with 50 guns. Built by Wigram & Green of Blackwall and launched February 21, 1814. Length 159 ft, beam 42 ft, 1,260 bm tons. Built in pitch-pine. Broken up at Chatham, work completed January, 1829

Granicus — *Captain William F Wise*
Fifth rate frigate armed with 36 guns. Built by Barton of Limehouse and launched October 25, 1813. Length 144 ft, beam 38 ft, 942 bm tons. Built in pitch-pine and carrying 14 x 32-pounder carronades and 28 x 18-pounder cannon. Sold to breakers in 1817

Hebrus — *Captain Edmund Palmer CB*
Fifth rate frigate armed with 36 guns. Built by Barton of Limehouse and launched September 13, 1813. Length 143 ft, beam 38 ft, 939 bm tons. Built in yellow pine and carrying 14 x 32-pounder carronades and 28 x 12-pounder cannon. Sold to J Cristall for breaking, April 1817

Heron — *Commander George Bentham**
Brig-sloop armed with 18 guns. *Cruizer* class, 387 bm tons. Built by King of Upnor and launched with the name *Rattlesnake* on October 22, 1812. Renamed *Heron* in 1813. Broken up in March, 1831

Mutine — *Commander James Mould*
Brig-sloop armed with 18 guns. *Cruizer* class, 386 bm tons. Built by Chapman of Bideford and launched August 15, 1806. Sold to G Young in February, 1819

Britomart — *Commander Robert Riddell*
Brig-sloop armed with 10 guns. Built by Dudman of Deptford and launched July 28, 1808. *Cherokee* class, 238 bm tons. (This vessel is listed also as having been built at Portsmouth Royal Dockyard) Sold to G Bailey, February 1819

Cordelia — *Commander William Sargent*
Brig-sloop armed with 10 guns. Built by King of Upnor and launched July 26, 1808. *Cherokee* class, 239 bm tons. Sold in December, 1833

Prometheus — *Commander William B Dashwood**
Brig-sloop armed with 16 guns. Built by Thompson of Southampton and launched March 27, 1807. Length 109 ft, beam 30 ft, 432 bm tons. Originally intended as a fire

ship but employed on normal duties such as convoy escort to Quebec (1812). Renamed *Veteran* in May, 1839 and broken up in August, 1852

Beelzebub — *Commander William Kempthorne*
Bomb armed with 8 guns and 2 mortars. Built by Taylor of Bideford and launched July 30, 1813. Length 102 ft, beam 27 ft, 334 bm tons.
Sold to breakers, work completed in September, 1820

Fury — *Commander Constantine R Moorsom**
Bomb armed with 8 guns and 2 mortars. Built by Ross of Rochester and launched April 4, 1814. Length 106 ft, beam 28 ft, 377 bm tons.
Converted to Arctic discovery in 1824, bilged in the ice in August, 1825, in Regent Inlet

Hecla — *Commander William Popham**
Bomb armed with 10 guns and one 13in mortar. Built by Barkworth & Hawkes of North Barton and launched on July 22, 1815. Length 105 ft, beam 29 ft, 375 bm tons.
Converted and sailed on Arctic discovery cruises between 1819 and 1827, and noted for services under Rear-Admiral Sir W E Parry RN. Sold in 1831

Infernal — *Commander the Hon George J Percival**
Bomb armed with 6 guns and one mortar. Built by Barkworth & Hawkes of North Barton and launched on July 26, 1815. Length 105 ft, beam 28 ft, 374 bm tons.
Sold to Mr Snook in April, 1831

Falmouth — *Thomas Armstrong, Master**
Schooner. Built at Topsham, Exeter, in 1807. Length 70 ft, beam 23 ft, 160 bm tons. Used for dockyard service in 1808. Converted into a mortar vessel in 1824. Converted into a dockyard lighter in 1846 and renamed *YC1*. Renamed again in 1870, *YC46*. Reverted to original name of *Falmouth* in 1870. Sold in 1883

Friends and **Maria**
Transports

Jasper — *Commander Thomas Carew*
Despatch vessel. Accompanied Lord Exmouth's squadron on the first part of his passage out from England, but sailed back from Gibraltar with his initial despatch and a copy of his intended plan of battle. Not present at the bombardment. Totally wrecked under Bear's Head (Plymouth Sound) in the great gale on the night of January 19, 1817, with the loss of 52 men and 15 women (2 men survived). Carew, ashore at the time, was acquitted by the Court Martial and subsequently married a widow lady with a fortune of £80,000

Fly — *John Lewis, Master (correct title, Patron)*
Buoy vessel ex-Gibraltar Dockyard, fitted out as an explosion vessel. Listed in some accounts as **Vesuvius**

Express — *Master's Mate Christopher Dale*
Tender to *Albion*: one of the small auxiliaries

The minor vessels

Gun boats *(ships' long-boats converted at Gibraltar)*

No 5 ex Queen Charlotte *Lieut Richard H Fleming** (also HMS Fly),
*Master's Mate William G H Wish** (promoted), *Midshipman Hon Charles P Yorke**

No 1 ex Impregnable *Lieut Matthew Munro**, *Midshipman Daniel Cox*

No 24 ex Superb *Lieut Robert B Johnstone**, *Midshipman William Mills*

No 23 ex Minden *Lieut Francis R Coghlan**, *Midshipman Charles G Grubb* (slightly wounded), *Midshipman John Sibley**

No 19 ex Albion *Lieut James Burton (B)**, *Midshipman John C Evison**

Rocket boats *(ships' flat boats converted at Gibraltar)*

Formed into two Divisions directed by *Lieut J T Fuller RHA** and
*Lieut J H Stevens RMA**

No 1 ex Queen Charlotte *Midshipman Robert H Baker* (wounded)
No 2 ex Impregnable *Master's Mate David J Burr*
No 3 ex Superb *Midshipman James G Raymond**
No 5 ex Minden *Second Master William Arthur*
No 4 ex Albion *Midshipman James Walmsley*, *Midshipman James Liddell**
No 7 ex Leander *Midshipman James Everard* (promoted)
No 6 ex Granicus *Master's Mate James Strong* (promoted), *Midshipman Edward Wynne*

No 8 ex Hebrus *Midshipman Aaron S Symes** (wounded, promoted),
Midshipman G H A Pocock (killed)

Gun boat yawls *(supplied ex Gibraltar Dockyard)*

No 1 ex Queen Charlotte *Master's Mate Edward Hillman* (promoted)
No 2 ex Queen Charlotte *Midshipman Alfred Sainthill** (promoted)
No 3 ex Impregnable *Midshipman John A Ball**
No 4 ex Impregnable *Master's Mate Thomas Woods**
No 5 ex Superb *Actg Lieut George W Cumming* (wounded, promoted)
No 6 ex Minden *Master's Mate Charles C Dent** (wounded, promoted)
No 7 ex Albion *Midshipman Alexander D Fordyce**
No 8 ex Albion *Midshipman Hill Wallace*
No 11 ex Leander *Midshipman James Bell*
No 12 ex Leander *Midshipman Charles B Ware** (promoted)
No 9 ex Severn *Midshipman Daniel McN Beatty** (wounded, promoted),
Midshipman James Foster (wounded)

No 13 ex Glasgow *Midshipman Robert J Cunningham*
No 14 ex Glasgow *Midshipman Elliott Morres**
No 10 ex Granicus *Midshipman Lewis T Jones** (slightly wounded),
*Midshipman John Garrett**

No 15 ex Hebrus *Midshipman George W Webber**
No 16 ex Hebrus *Midshipman James Creagh** (promoted)

Mortar boats *(ships' launches converted at Gibraltar)*

No 1 ex Queen Charlotte *Lieut Ambrose A R Wolrige RMA**,
Actg Lieut George Hales (promoted)

No 2 ex Impregnable *Lieut Theophilus Beauchant RMA**,
Master's Mate John Holberton* (promoted)

No 3 ex Superb *Master's Mate Andrew Barclay, Midshipman Frederick A Wilkinson**

No 4 ex Minden *Lieut W Oliver Aitchison RMA, Midshipman John Ahern*
No 5 ex Albion *Midshipman William B Lamb* (promoted),
Midshipman Parker D Bingham*

No 8 ex Leander *Midshipman T W Ashington* (died of wounds 21.9.16)
No 6 ex Severn *Master's Mate William Ryder** (promoted), *Midshipman J A Bainbridge*

No 9 ex Glasgow *Midshipman Edward H Pace**
No 7 ex Granicus *Master's Mate Edmund R Marley, Midshipman John Munro*
No 10 ex Hebrus *Master's Mate John Sanderson*, Midshipman Arthur Barnes*

Gun boat barges *(supplied ex Gibraltar Dockyard)*

No 1 ex Queen Charlotte *Midshipman John Rivett-Carnac** (promoted)
No 2 ex Queen Charlotte *Midshipman Henry McClintock* (promoted)
No 3 ex Queen Charlotte *Midshipman George Markham* (wounded)
No 4 ex Impregnable *Midshipman Benjamin Hayter**
No 5 ex Impregnable *Midshipman C T C Hookham*
No 6 ex Superb *Master's Mate Francis Barrs* (promoted)
No 7 ex Minden *Midshipman William Hornby**
No 8 ex Minden *Midshipman Thomas Marriott* (promoted)
No 9 ex Albion *Midshipman John Radcliff** (promoted)
No 10 ex Albion *Master's Mate William Y Gill**
No 11 ex Albion *Midshipman John Cheape*
No 14 ex Leander *Master's Mate Edward Aitchison* (wounded, promoted)
No 12 ex Severn *Midshipman James Bolton*, Midshipman E C Miller*
No 15 ex Glasgow *Midshipman William Radcliffe** (promoted)
No 13 ex Granicus *Midshipman Thomas B Wells*, Midshipman William Hamilton*

No 16 ex Hebrus *Midshipman Michael Turner**

---

a: up to 1873 the tonnage of a vessel was calculated by the 'builder's measurement' (bm), a measurement of hull capacity arrived at by calculating the number of tuns (casks) of wine which a ship could carry. This standard probably originated in the fifteenth century. After 1873 the 'displacement tonnage' was adopted and then, in 1926, 'standard displacement'.

b: the length shown for each ship is the length of the main gun deck.

c: the rate shown for the battleships and frigates is not a reflection upon the quality of the vessel but indicates the rates of pay and allowances for the Captains of such ships.

d: where more than one name appears for a particular vessel, the officer first named was the one who commanded during the battle

e: all officers listed above were Royal Navy unless otherwise indicated

f: an asterisk indicates that the officer lived long enough to claim and receive a Naval General Service medal with the clasp ALGIERS (and possibly other action clasps if he was so eligible)

g: 'promoted' signifies that the officer was promoted as a direct consequence of his service during the expedition.

Melampus — *Captain Antony-Willem De-Man*
A frigate of 40 guns. Formerly HMS *Melampus,* bought by the Dutch Government from the Royal Navy in 1815

Frederica — *Captain Jakob-Adrien Van-der-Straaten*
A frigate of 40 guns. Her full name was *Prinses Frederika Sophia Wilhelmina,* possibly the longest warship's name in maritime history, but shown in most accounts as simply the *Frederika*

Diana — *Captain Pietrus Zievogel*
A frigate of 40 guns. Formerly HMS *Diana,* bought by the Dutch Government from the Royal Navy in 1815

Amstel — *Captain Willem-Augustus Vanderhart*
A frigate of 40 guns

Dageraad — *Captain Johannes-Martinus Polders*
A frigate of 30 guns

Eendraght — *Captain Johannes-Frederik-Christian Wardenburg*
A corvette of 18 guns

THE ROCKET BRIGADE

THE PART PLAYED by the Rocket Brigade during the bombardment of Algiers was not vital but is certainly of historical interest. As can be seen from the general account of the action, arrangements had been made at Gibraltar for a 'flat boat' from each of the eight larger ships and frigates to be fitted out as rocket boats. This involved the installation of a rudimentary framework which supported the missiles at the correct angle of elevation prior to ignition.

The rockets used at Algiers had been designed some years earlier by William Congreve. This soldier-inventor was the eldest son of Lieutenant General Sir William Congreve, Colonel Commandant of the Royal Artillery, Comptroller of the Royal Laboratory at Woolwich and Superintendent of Military Machines. The younger William was born in 1772, passed through the Royal Academy at Woolwich, and entered the Royal Artillery as a second lieutenant in 1791. He was at once attached to the Royal Laboratory and began work under the supervision of his father. By 1804 he had produced a form of rocket, promptly named Congreve's rocket, which was reasonably reliable. The War office and the Board of Ordnance, doubtless impressed by his father's strong recommendations, decided to adopt the design.

Congreve's prime contribution to the advancement of rocketry was to abandon paper and wood as manufacturing materials. He replaced them with iron. The use of metal increased the weight of the missile but it also permitted the use of more powerful propellants which increased range, hitting power and stability in flight. Like his predecessors, Congreve worked initially on designs which would be used to set fire to an enemy's ships, towns and flammable stores. However, he found that the heavier iron-cased rockets could be made to carry an effective war-head. There were three basic types: shell, shrapnel and case-shot. He developed five different weights of missile, each intended for a different purpose but all having a range comparable with that of the conventional artillery of the day,

Weight of rocket	Maximum range
6-pounder	2,000 yards
9-pounder	2,250 yards
12-pounder	2,500 yards
32-pounder	2,750 yards
42-pounder	3,000 yards

He experimented with even larger rockets, weighing up to four hundred pounds, but the propellants at his disposal were not sufficiently powerful.

As a 'general purpose' weapon he settled on the 32-pounder as being the most satisfactory. For short-range use it could be launched in a near-horizontal position. When launched at an elevation of fifty-five degrees it could travel nearly three thousand yards, but much depended upon the strength and direction of the wind, atmospheric humidity and the condition of the propellant charge. This GP rocket consisted of a case which was 3ft 6in in length and 4in in diameter and was stabilised in flight by a stick 15ft in length!

Congreve's design was first used in action on October 18, 1806, when a squadron of eighteen British boats launched two hundred rockets into the port of Boulogne, starting a number of fires. It was used again at Copenhagen in 1807 and during the action at the Basque Roads in 1809. The results did not match expectations but they were good enough to justify further development. Authorisation was given for two Rocket Companies to be formed within the Corps of Royal Artillery.

In 1813 he was ordered to the Continent with the 2nd Rocket Company and took part in the Battle of Leipzig. The rockets did not do much material damage to the enemy but, according to a subsequent account, 'their noise and bright glare had a great effect in frightening the French and throwing them into confusion'.

The rockets were used in the Peninsula, at the forcing of the Bidassoa, where again they caused little damage but did spread terror amongst the enemy troops because of their novelty. Wellington was unimpressed. He complained that the missiles were inaccurate and 'frightened the horses'. The criticism regarding accuracy was undoubtedly valid. The same problem had arisen when the rockets were employed during the war with America in 1812.

Although Congreve ceased to be directly connected with the Rocket Companies after his appointment as Comptroller at Woolwich, his brainchild continued to prosper. Trial and error had shown the rockets to be most effective when fired in salvo and at targets which did not require great precision of aim. As late as 1827, Congreve was propounding his theory that rockets would replace conventional artillery, a remarkable forecast of things to come. His main argument related to the lightness and mobility of the weapon compared with the great weight of conventional cannon which needed large teams of horses and men.

In June, 1815, the British Army faced Napoleon for the last time, at Waterloo, and a small detachment of the Rocket Brigade was there to try again. It was commanded by Major Edward Charles Whinyates, Royal Artillery, a passionate advocate of the rocket.

Whinyates managed to fire a number of rockets during the action at Quatre Bras and succeeded in damaging a French cannon there. The Duke of Wellington gave specific orders that the Rocket Brigade troops should abandon their equipment and be dispersed to supplement the conventional artillerymen. A staff officer suggested that this would break Whinyates' heart. 'Damn his heart, Sir, let my order be obeyed', replied the Duke. Nothing had happened to change the view which he had formed in Spain.

Major Whinyates, however, was a resourceful man. Ignoring his Commander-in-Chief's wishes, he succeeded in bringing his men forward during the morning of June 18 and took them down into the valley somewhere to the front of La Haye Sainte. Such swift movement across country was easy because the rocketeers were mounted. Each man carried a light launching frame made of iron and a number of six-pounder rockets in a leather sling-harness. The rockets were duly set up in a field, pointed in the appropriate direction, and sent on their way. They had no discernible effect upon the French but Whinyates, who had three horses shot from under him during the day, received a severe wound in the arm. There was also a strong complaint from the Household Cavalry. He had launched his salvo just as the cavalrymen were making a dashingly magnificent charge and it was felt that his infernal contraptions had lowered the tone of the proceedings.

The decision, taken two years later, to send a rocket detachment to Algiers, was based upon three suppositions: the Dey's native infantry would be terrified by a weapon which they had never previously experienced, the town of Algiers would be set alight, and the Algerine ships would be burned at their moorings.

The first of these suppositions proved groundless because, although initially startled, the defenders maintained a brave and determined resistance throughout the battle. The second supposition also was not justified because the Algerine houses were built entirely of masonry. The North African coast had been stripped of woodland many centuries before and there was simply no timber available for building purposes. Hence the town could not burn.

Where the rockets did prove their value was on shipping in the harbour. The Algerine fleet was destroyed almost totally by fire and there can be little doubt that Congreve's invention was in large part responsible. The ballistic missile was no longer a spectacular novelty, it was now an effective item of weaponry.

The Congreve-designed rockets remained in service for a remarkably long time. They underwent various modifications, intended to improve their stability in flight, but it was 1866 before they were declared obsolete. A mechanic employed at the Royal Arsenal, William Hale, had invented a new type of rocket in 1845. Ignored by the Board of Ordnance, he took his missiles to America where he demonstrated them to officers of the US army and navy at Washington, in January, 1847. Further successful trials were held at the Washington Arsenal. Twenty years later the Hale design was accepted into service by the British army and Royal Navy, and Congreve's rocket faded into history.

SMUGGLERS AND POACHERS

DURING THE eighteenth and early nineteenth centuries smuggling was a major industry in the United Kingdom. The loss of revenue to the national exchequer was immense and Parliament devoted much time and thought to the prevention and punishment of smuggling offences. One of the measures taken to suppress these activities was the passing of a draconian Act (1805) which ordered the automatic impressment of anyone found in a vessel engaged in smuggling. In other words, if an officer of the Customs Service, (or the Army, Royal Navy or Royal Marines) had cause to arrest a man alleged to be engaged in smuggling, or travelling as passenger in a smuggling vessel, then that officer immediately and directly delivered his prisoner into a Royal Navy ship or to the nearest jail. The men then had a period of thirty days in which to contact a lawyer (not an easy thing to do in the circumstances) and to seek an appearance before magistrates. If he failed to do this, or if he was found guilty, the automatic sentence was a minimum of five years' impressment.

Three ships of the Royal Navy have been named HMS Algiers in commemoration of the 1816 battle. This is the single screw ship HMS Algiers of 1854 (National Maritime Museum)

The only exceptions were men who were physically unfit for sea service: these went to court and then to prison as common criminals. In practice, many smugglers were prime experienced mariners and they made a welcome addition to a ship's muster list.

As we know (Chapter 5), it was the C-in-C Plymouth who first suggested that Exmouth's manning problems could be solved in part by the delivery to his squadron of all smugglers then in custody at Plymouth, Portsmouth and the Nore. The Admiralty immediately issued the appropriate orders and fifty prime crewmen were added to the expedition as a consequence. Thirty-two went to *Minden*, nineteen to *Impregnable* and five to *Superb*. Some idea of the fine quality of these men may be gained from the following description of two smugglers who succeeded in escaping from *Queen Charlotte* in the early hours of June 29, 1816, as she lay in Portsmouth harbour,

John White alias Oliver: fair complexion, brown hair, grey eyes, 5ft 11in tall (an immense height for the period, the tallest Royal Marines being 5ft 9in), high bred, a fisherman, 15 years at sea, born Portland, age 25.

William Webb: swarthy complexion, dark hair, dark eyes, 5ft 6in tall, stout make, dark frizzed short hair, whiskers full face, much freckled and spotted, a fisherman, 5 years at sea, born Weymouth, age 24.

They both evaded the expedition to Barbary, but John Oliver was recaptured by a police officer at Weymouth and sent back to Spithead in September. Meanwhile the other smugglers had been through a more exciting adventure than even smuggling could offer.

Lord Exmouth's basic humanity and precision of mind led to yet another of his post-battle reports to the Admiralty,

> *'Queen Charlotte* at sea. 12th September, 1816
> With reference to my letter No 63 in which I recommended to Their Lordships mercy to the Smugglers now serving in the Squadron under my Command, and expressed my intention of bringing them home for Their Lordships disposal, I beg to state to you that this determination has been strengthened by the uniform reports that have been made to me of the good conduct of these brave men by the Captains of their respective Ships to which they were attached during the attack on Algiers.
> I am fully sensible that in adopting this line of proceeding I am acting in opposition to the intention of Their Lordships. I trust to their liberality for

forgiveness, as I cannot resist the inclination I feel to solicit this act of grace towards men who have behaved so admirably under my own immediate observation.

It is my intention to bring the whole of the smugglers home in the *Queen Charlotte*, and I request to receive their Lordships instructions respecting them on my arrival at Spithead.'

The relevant point here is the reference to bringing the smugglers home to England. The spirit of the Act, as interpreted by the Admiralty, indicated that the five years of impressment should be served in distant waters. It is probable that Exmouth was unaware of the full wording of the original Act which laid down that any officer who 'shall knowingly and wilfully permit a smuggler to evade the service intended by the Act, on conviction for any such offence either by court martial, or any information filed by His Majesty's Attorney General, shall be cashiered'. The Admiralty understood the implications and sent a gentle warning,

'Acquaint His Lordship that however the Board do much appreciate the conduct of the men, it is to Their Lordships regret that you have taken the step mentioned. His Lordship was probably not aware that these men are not serving in the Fleet under ordinary employment, or by Authority of this Board, but by the express provision of comments by Parliament which sentences such men to 5 years to be served at sea, and Their Lordships much doubt whether they or any other Power in the Country can legally discharge these men. Their Lordships will however lose no time in obtaining the opinion of the Law Officers of the Crown on this point, but Their Lordships must add that even if the Law on this subject were clear, then Their Lordships would not have taken this step without a previous communication with the Treasury and Revenue Departments.'

Legal opinion was solemnly consulted, the matter being examined by the office of His Majesty's Attorney and Solicitor General and the council for the affairs of the Admiralty and Navy. They wasted no time and, by October 7, two days before Exmouth's triumphal return to London, an ingenious solution to the problem had been drafted in Lincolns Inn,

'We have considered the question which has been submitted to us on the recommendation from Lord Exmouth, that the smugglers on board His Lordship's Fleet, should be discharged, in consequence of the admirable conduct of these brave Men under his Lordship's own immediate observation, and we are of the opinion that if it shall be thought proper to mark the late splendid transaction by such an act of grace, as a reward to the Men for their good conduct, the proper mode of doing so would be, if His Royal Highness the Prince Regent, shall be pleased so to order, to grant to the men recommended His Majesty's free pardon, which in its terms would remit all pains and penalties and punishments, and thereupon it would be competent for the Lords of the Admiralty to order their discharge from the Service.'

This encouraging response was followed by further discussions and the wheels were set in motion for a Royal Pardon to be drafted. At this point the lawyers suddenly woke up to the fact that Parliament had already anticipated their dilemma by passing an Act, on July 30, 1814, which permitted the Treasury to mitigate and remit any penalties incurred under the laws of Customs and Excise. The warning to Exmouth had not been necessary. The Admiralty's legal advisers had not done their homework properly.

Further enquiries were raised concerning the behaviour of the fifty smugglers and the six poachers during the expedition. Reports were submitted in respect of the crimes for which they were originally arrested. The bulky dossiers were passed from one desk to another until finally it was agreed that 'their former offences had not been of so daring a nature as to make their further detention absolutely necessary'. Each smuggler was asked to make his mark on a document by which he bound himself 'not to be again concerned in smuggling'. Similar arrangements were made in respect of the poachers. The Treasury duly authorised the Admiralty to release the men, the first batch being set free on December 14, 1816, the last on January 30, 1817. They did not receive the two months' gratuity paid out to all the other men in Exmouth's squadron, but they did receive their basic pay.

The practice of sending civil offenders to serve their sentences in ships of the Royal Navy continued until 1834. The last of these impressed men were released in 1837 and the majority had served five years in distant waters. The men who sailed with Exmouth, however, had served less than a year of impressed time (some served only six or seven months). The special dispensation granted in their case was yet another reflection of the nation's enthusiasm for the victory at Algiers.

It is a curious fact that a high proportion of these men (ten of the fifty smugglers and three of the six poachers) lived long enough to claim their medals in 1849.

ROYAL MARINES AND
ROYAL MARINE ARTILLERY

LORD EXMOUTH'S original battle plan, issued on August 6, 1816, contained the following instructions with regard to the employment of the Marines,

The Marines to be put into two battalions to be commanded by two senior officers when landed.

	1st Battalion	2nd Battalion	
Queen Charlotte	170	150	Impregnable
Superb	125	125	Minden
Leander	84	125	Albion
Severn	64	64	Glasgow
Granicus	48	48	Hebrus
Totals	491	512	

Each three-decker will form her party into 4 Divisions
Each two-decker will form her party into 3 Divisions
Each frigate will form her party into 2 Divisions
Whenever one Division is ordered to land from each ship the appointed Officer will take his Command
If the 1st and 2nd Divisions are ordered to land the Captains will in this case land with them, taking the 2nd subalterns and leave the Seniors aboard
Major Vallack to land in Command of the 1st and 2nd Divisions, and Major Collins to command the remaining party whenever they may be ordered to land
Lieut Hunt of the Queen Charlotte will act as Adjutant and four steady men from each Division are to be selected to carry rockets and storming poles
The C-in-C sees in the intended attack a possibility of pushing on the Mole the First and possibly the 2nd Divisions of Marines from each ship, under cover of their own ships, in order to support the Sappers and Miners who will land with them.
The Flat Boats and Launches therefore to be used as Gun and Rocket Boats under the shelter of and close to the ship to which they belong, ready to take advantage of any sudden confusion of the enemy by embarking a Division in each of the two

boats. They will assemble alongside the Flag Ship there to receive orders when the signal 3AC is made.

The men to land without any encumbrance with sixty rounds of ammunition and canteens if they have any, and a proportion of small rockets (*sic*) will be distributed among them for throwing into the casements.'

No such landing took place but we have various eye-witness accounts of the part played by some of the officers during the bombardment.

Lieutenants Robert Henry, John Maule, H James and James Bisset, all of the Royal Marine Artillery, were responsible for the operation of the mortars aboard the four bomb vessels (*Beelzebub, Fury, Hecla* and *Infernal*). Upon their return to England, the survivors were each required to submit detailed reports and suggestions regarding any possible improvements. It was noted that *Fury* had fired off twice as many shells as the three other vessels. This resulted in extensive enquiries into the methods of handling the shells, bringing them up from the hold to the mortar, preparing the fuses, and so forth. Exmouth, in his despatch, wrote, 'the shells from the bombs were admirably well thrown directly across and over us. Not an accident that I know of occurred to any ship'.

James Bisset, aboard the *Infernal,* had a strong presentiment of his own death long before the fleet reached Algiers. He told his friends several times that 'he would be one of the first'. Events proved him correct. The bombardment had barely begun, and Bisset was supervising the loading of the fifth shell, when he was struck by an Algerine shot. Another officer witnessed his death, 'he seemed calmly waiting with the cool yet determined resolution of a gallant spirit who knows his last hour has come. I could never imagine what sort of missile it was that ended his mortal career. He was cut in three pieces. One leg went forward on the gangway, and the other, and part of his body, remained nearly where he had been standing. His upper works went over-board. Certainly on that day the Algerines threw about some queer articles, such as crow-bars, iron bolts, hand-spikes, glass bottles, bags of nails, etc, *ad libitum*'.

A lance corporal named Polter fired all the other shots from *Infernal* that day.

Captain and Brevet Major A Gillespie, the first historian of the Marine Corps, was serving on board *Albion*. At the time of the action he was suffering so severely from gout that he was unable to stand. He refused to remain below and was carried up on deck in a chair where he remained seated throughout the battle, cheering his men on! He was not injured, but the episode proved too much for his constitution and on his return to England he was invalided out of the service.

Captain James Willson, commanding the *Leander's* detachment, was mortally injured by a ball which smashed both his legs. The surgeons started to operate and were amputating his legs when he saw nearby one of his men, Sergeant Brabazon, who had just lost an arm. 'Ah, Brabazon, are you here? I am sorry to see you thus. This is a glorious work above, we are not unavenged'. Willson remained conscious and cheerful until he died a few minutes later.

Captain Willson's second in command, Lieutenant George Baxter, was one of the first men to die in the battle, being shot through the head by a musket ball.

After the battle Lord Exmouth wrote to Sir Richard Williams of the Royal Marine Artillery, 'I should be very ungrateful, my dear friend, if I neglected to thank you for the care you took in selecting for the service I was ordered upon the best officers and men I ever saw during my service. Indeed, my dear Sir Richard, you proved yourself a real and sincere friend to me. Captain Burton, poor fellow, has been wounded; he was a treasure to me in every respect. One very fine fellow has been killed (Lieutenant Bisset) and I can assure you that all the officers did you full justice — they all knew their duty and performed it well.'

Marine casualties at Algiers were: five officers and twenty other ranks killed, three officers and one hundred and four other ranks wounded.

GUNS AND GUNNERY

THERE WERE SEVERAL novel developments in the sphere of weaponry at the bombardment of Algiers. The principal innovations are listed below:

1: *Fynmore's Quill Tubes*
The cannon of Exmouth's day were fired by a mechanism very similar to that used on the flintlock musket. A spring-loaded arm, fitted with a flint, struck a spark which ignited the priming powder which then in turn ignited the charge in the barrel. The difficulties of handling priming powder aboard ship, contending with the wind and spray coming in through the gun ports, are easy to imagine. It is particularly interesting, therefore, to discover the following comments in a report written to the Admiralty in October, 1816, by Captain Edmund Palmer CB, of the frigate *Hebrus*,

'Before I close this report, I beg to state for Their Lorships information that on the passage to Algiers Lieutenant James Fynmore of the Royal Marines embarked in the *Hebrus*, made a tube of a certain composition, which upon tryal (*sic*) was found to answer so perfectly, and to be so superior to the Tube furnished HM Ships, that I was induced to send some of them to the Commander in Chief, who was pleased to approve of them most highly.

These Tubes were furnished to several of the ships engaged and answered so completely that I have thought it right with the approval of Lord Exmouth, to transmit for Their Lordships inspection some of them which are in a box that accompanies this letter. Their superiority over the old Tube consists in this.

The old Tube, after being fixed in the touch-hole of the gun, requires to be primed in the usual manner with common priming powder, and it is necessary this priming should explode before the tube itself can ignite. This priming upon which the Tube entirely depends, is ever liable to suffer from wet, or to be blown away at the instant it is flung open by the flint, an occurrence that frequently occasions the greatest inconvenience.

Now, in this new Tube, there is no occasion for any priming whatever with loose powder. The space in the pan is filled by a lock of worsted identified with and growing out of the Tube, and prepared in a composition so subtile (*sic*) in its nature, that if but the smallest spark is emitted from the flint the effect is certain and instantaneous.

In transmitting these Tubes, I beg to add that I have found Lieut Fynmore upon all occasions, as upon this, to be a zealous good Officer, observant of everything tending to the benefit of HM Service.

Palmer'

The Admiralty conferred with William Congreve at the Royal Laboratory. Congreve suggested some minor improvements but approved the principle.

'Nov 15. Write to Lieut James Fynmore and state to him that Their Lordships having made trial of this innovation were satisfied that its principle is highly useful. That they have directed it to be brought into general use in the service, and as a mark of their approbation of his experiments & zeal, they have directed me to have a piece of plate to the value of 100 guineas prepared and given to him with a suitable inscription.'

We may well ponder the fact that it required just three weeks for the authorities to receive Captain Palmer's report, to conduct the trials, make the improvements and approve the adoption of the device throughout the Royal Navy. They had even decided upon an appropriate level of reward for the young officer (he was later asked if he would prefer to have 100 guineas in money instead of silver plate). It is unlikely that the decision-making process could operate quite so smoothly in the present day.

2: *Congreve's Carronades*

Carronades took their name from the town of Carron in Scotland where they were first manufactured in 1777. Short-barrelled short-range weapons, they had a devastating effect in muzzle to muzzle encounters. To the gunners they were known as 'smashers'. They were ideal for Exmouth's purpose at Algiers, subject to the proviso (which he succeeded in meeting) of manoeuvering his ships to within a very short distance of the targets.

Congreve had been working upon a new improved type and several were carried by *Queen Charlotte*. Carronades of a more conventional type were carried in many of the other ships in Exmouth's squadron and, upon their return to England, each of the ships' captains was instructed to submit a full report to the Admiralty regarding the performance of the weapons. They were of varying calibres: 18, 24, 32 and 68-pounders, up to 8 feet in length and weighing 4700 pounds. Depending upon the type of target engaged, and depending upon the personal preference of the gunnery officer, they fired single shot ball, double-shotted ball, ball and canister, and ball and grape. The varying combinations of load, backed with varying charges of powder, produced a variety of results. The post-battle analysis generated a voluminous correspondence, as the gunnery experts gave their opinions concerning possible additional improvements in design and operation. It was the consensus view that Colonel Sir William Congreve's carronade had performed exceedingly well at Algiers.

There was also much interest in Exmouth's idea of hoisting 12-pounder carronades up into the cross-trees aboard *Queen Charlotte* and *Severn*. It was these weapons which, loaded with grape, blasted the Algerine gunners on the top tier of the mole-head battery. As late as August 21 Exmouth had set the carpenters to work, extemporising a recoil slide which could be lashed to the foretop. It was test fired aboard *Severn* with full load and, as soon as the trial had proved successful, similar slides were made for the maintop, also for the cross-trees of *Queen Charlotte*. It was typical of Exmouth: planning ahead, using new ideas, testing them thoroughly before going into battle.

3: *Mortar boats*

On November 6, 1816, all post captains returned from Algiers were ordered to report upon the mortar boats, how they had been fitted out and how they had performed in action. The flagship's captain, Sir James Brisbane, received his copy of the enquiry while on leave at Eashing House, Godalming, and he passed it on to his warrant carpenter, William Strong. The reply gives a revealing insight into the stolid professionalism of an old sailor in an age when very few were literate,

Queen Charlotte 12th November, 1816

'Sir James,
In reply to your letter of the 8th instant, the first preparation in the Launch for the reception of the Howitzer was four 3 inch plank, 10 inch wide & 10 foot long, two on each side of Keelson, fastened with screws over the ceiling to the timbers, with diminishing stuff as high up on the floors as was necessary to admit the size of the platform or bed, — and the 3 inch fir plank with the diminishing stuff was twice lined over, once thwartship and once fore and aft with ¾ elm board then stowed with black ochum stuffed in canvas bags, so as to make it level to take the platform before the platform was placed on it. It was all covered over with a tarpauling naile

round & well secured. To prevent fire the platform was made of 3 inch fir & lined very strong, screw ring bolt at each corner, a screw eye-bolt at midship fore & after end to secure it to the keelson, — to two screw eye bolts screwed in there for that purpose, four additional screw rings bolts was put in the flooring, that is two of each side for securing the howitzer & two screw ring bolts each side of the boat in the gunwall for train tackles.

The launch was shot through in the Action two feet before the stern at the water edge, in filling she turns over and came bottom up, the Howitzer being well secured was prevented from falling out. I found it secure in the Launch the next morning & was then got safe in the ship. The launch bore the concussion of the Howitzer firing below the water very well, the upper seams of ochum was shook out, but no plank or butt started.

The above is as nigh as I can recollect Sir James.

I remain etc etc Wm Strong'

The boats so equipped were ship's pulling boats, thirty feet in length. They were certainly never intended to absorb the shock of discharge from a mortar firing a shell, eight inches diameter, over a distance of a mile and propelled by three pounds of explosive. And yet, with only lengths of timber and bags of oakum, the carpenters were able to put Exmouth's ideas into immediate effect, increasing the fleet's fire-power considerably.

5: *Gunsights*

In January, 1814, Captain Arthur Farquhar RN, commanding the Heligoland Squadron, aided a detachment of the Swedish Army at the investment of a powerful fortress at Gluckstadt on the River Elbe. The nature of the fighting called for particularly accurate gun-laying. Farquhar concluded that the sights fitted to the Royal Navy's cannon were inadequate and, upon his return to England, he designed a new type. He passed his invention to the Board of Ordnance and it was agreed that trials should be made.

This decision coincided with Exmouth's departure for Algiers and the Admiralty swiftly arranged with the Board of Ordnance for six of the experimental brass sights to be sent to Portsmouth. They were shown to Lord Exmouth who conducted trials of his own during the passage south to Gibraltar. Fitted to the Congreve carronade on *Queen Charlotte*'s quarterdeck, and tested against Lieutenant Crichdon's novel practice target, they produced an astonishing improvement in accuracy of aim. Exmouth set his carpenters to work manufacturing wooden replicas of the brass prototypes and, by the time the squadron reached the Mediterranean, every single cannon and carronade in the squadron had been modified.

The ships' captains were not specifically requested to submit post-battle reports on the sights, but Captain Ekins of the *Superb* volunteered the information that 'they were soon understood (by the guns' crews) and were very serviceable.' Exmouth commented favourably upon them in his final report to the Admiralty.

A study of the letters and reports written after the battle leads us to certain conclusions. First, even though Great Britain had been at war almost continuously between 1793 and 1814, the design and operation of cannon had still not been perfected. Secondly, men such as Exmouth and Congreve were aware of the deficiencies and were prepared to continue with new experiments despite the return of peace and the removal of wartime pressures. Thirdly, Exmouth's expedition did not consist simply of a group of vessels sailing away, bombarding an enemy port and then sailing home again to enjoy the glory and acclaim. There was far more to it than that. Every officer engaged was required to submit detailed reports, to offer his own views and criticisms of the equipment used, and to be a thinking individual. Fourthly, any experimental item which gave satisfactory

The Dutch commemorated the battle by naming one of their warships Algiers. She is depicted here in Marseilles roads. In 1828 she was renamed Sambre (Naval Historical Dept, The Hague)

service in battle was adopted immediately into general use and the inventor rewarded for his initiative.

The British industrial revolution had not yet moved into high gear, but we can perhaps detect in the methods of the Royal Navy that belief in technical innovation and aggressive management which soon was to change the face of the country.

Summary of munitions expended

Queen Charlotte	30,424 lbs powder	4,462 round shot
Impregnable	28,800 lbs powder	6,730 round shot
Superb	23,200 lbs powder	4,500 round shot
Minden	24,536 lbs powder	4,710 round shot
Albion	22,520 lbs powder	4,110 round shot
Leander	21,700 lbs powder	3,680 round shot
Severn	12,910 lbs powder	2,920 round shot
Granicus	13,460 lbs powder	3,000 round shot
Hebrus	9,960 lbs powder	2,800 round shot
Totals	84.00 tons powder	36,912 round shot

1: the disproportionate returns for *Impregnable* reflect the fact that she was firing double-shotted for much of the time

2: the Five Dutch vessels discharged 10,148 round shot

3: in addition to the above figures there was the expenditure of mortar shells by the four bomb vessels, armed with 10in and 13in mortars manned by the Royal Marine Artillery:

Fury	318 shells
Hecla	152 shells
Beelzebub	160 shells and 20 carcasses
	(incendiary projectiles)
Infernal	180 shells and 6 carcasses

4:   there are no official returns for the number of Congreve rockets launched, but it is evident that several hundred were used and they were mainly of the 32-pounder general purpose type

5:   in addition to the reports of round shot fired there was a substantial expenditure in grape and canister shot. The total expenditure may be estimated at 100 tons of powder and 500 tons of shot

ALGIERS — A SELECTED BIBLIOGRAPHY

Edward Pellew — Viscount Exmouth, Admiral of the Red
C Northcote Parkinson· Methuen 1934

Knight of the Sword — Life and letters of Sir Sidney Smith
Lord Russell of Liverpool· Victor Gollancz 1964

Naval biographical dictionary
William R O'Byrne· John Murray 1849 and 1863

The life of Nelson
Capt A T Mahan· Sampson Low Marston 1898

The naval history of Great Britain
William James· Richard Bentley 1878

They saw it happen 1689-1897
T Charles-Edwards and Brian Richardson· Basil Blackwell 1958

Medals of the British Navy and how they were won
W H Long· Norie & Wilson 1895

Dawn like thunder — the Barbary wars and the birth of the US Navy
Glenn Tucker· Bobbs Merrill (USA) 1963

Our Navy and the Barbary Corsairs
Gardner W Allen· Houghton Mifflin (USA) 1909

The Sultan's Admiral — the life of Barbarossa
Ernle Bradford· Hodder & Stoughton 1969

The Barbary slaves
Stephen Clissold· Purnell Book Services 1977

Corsairs of Malta and Barbary
Peter Earle· Sidgwick & Jackson 1970

Nest of Corsairs
Seton Dearden· John Murray 1976

Bibliography of Algiers (Royal Geographical Society — Vol II Part 2)
Lt Col Sir John L Playfair· John Murray 1888

Britain's sea soldiers
Col Cyril Field RMLI · The Lyceum Press 1924

A narrative of the expedition to Algiers in the year 1816
A Salamé · John Murray 1819

Thanks voted by the House of Lords and the House of Commons to the Army and Navy (1801-1859)
Henry Hansard 1859

The Naval Chronicle
1816 and 1817

Royal Naval biography
John Marshall · Longman (all volumes 1823-1835)

Lives of Admiral Penrose and Captain Trevenen
Rev John Penrose · John Murray 1850

English corsairs on the Barbary coast
Christopher Lloyd · Collins 1981

The Croker papers (Vol I)
Louis J Jennings · John Murray 1884

Algiers
Cdr F C van Oosten, Royal Netherlands Navy · Marineblad 1966

The life of Admiral Viscount Exmouth
Edward Osler · Smith Elder 1835

The Barbary corsairs
S Lane Poole · Fisher Unwin 1890

Naval warfare
Rear-Admiral P H Colomb 1891

Naval Battles from 1744 to the peace of 1814
Rear-Admiral Charles Ekins · Baldwin, Cradock and Joy 1824

Sketches of Algiers
William Shaler, 1826

SOURCES

Selected original sources at the Public Records Office — ADM 1/- series: Commanders-in-Chief, Admirals', Captains', Lieutenants', and Promiscuous Letters. Minutes. Royal Marines. Ordnance. ADM 7/- series: Admiralty Board Journals, Acts of Parliament — Prevention of Smuggling (from GEO I to WILL IV). ADM 12/- series: Admiralty Digest Books. ADM 37/- series: Ships' Muster Lists. ADM 51/- series: Captains' Logs. ADM 53/- series: Masters' Logs. Treasury T/28 and T/29. Foreign Office FO 3/- series: Correspondence with Admiralty. War Office WO 54/-, 61/-, 97/: Ordnance, Sappers & Miners and Rocket Troop. Also London Gazette and Gibraltar Gazette.

Index

THE PEOPLE

THE SHIPS

**Where the name of a person or ship appears in a caption,
the relevant page number appears here in bold numerals.**

200